Media Education and the (Re)Production of Culture

Critical Studies in Education and Culture Series

NICOLAS DE BASILY

Diplomat of Imperial Russia

1903-1917

MEMOIRS

Hoover Institution Press
Stanford University
Stanford, California

The Hoover Institution on War, Revolution and Peace, founded at Stanford University in 1919 by the late President Herbert Hoover, is a center for advanced study and research on public and international affairs in the twentieth century. The views expressed in its publications are entirely those of the authors and do not necessarily reflect the views of the staff, officers, or Board of Overseers of the Hoover Institution.

Hoover Institution Publications 125
International Standard Book Number 0–8179–1251–7
Library of Congress Catalog Card Number 70–175450
© 1973 by the Board of Trustees of the
    Leland Stanford Junior University
All rights reserved
Printed in the United States of America

Table of Contents

Foreword

In 1964 the Hoover Institution received from Mrs. Lascelle de Basily the personal papers of her late husband, Nicolas de Basily, a prominent Russian diplomat. In addition to unique documentation concerning the abdication of Tsar Nicholas II of Russia, these papers contained Basily's personal reminiscences, in French, written some time during his residence in France, Uruguay, and the United States.

The memoirs include a colorful description of Basily's youth and early career as a diplomat. They also present a knowledgeable and highly informative account of political development in Russia which led to the Tsar's abdication from the vantage point of Imperial Army Headquarters during the first critical days of March 1917 (or last days of February according to the Gregorian calendar). These reminiscences are considerably more detailed than most of the narratives written by other actors or observers in the final drama of Russia and the Romanovs. This is so in part because Basily's official position during those days provided him with extraordinary insights as the crisis developed. The Duma leaders at Petrograd, who had created a Provisional Government for Russia even before the Tsar abdicated, were aware of the charged political atmosphere and the revolutionary situation in the capital. This intelligence convinced the generals that they should persuade the Emperor to abdicate in favor of his son and heir to the throne, Alexis. From published memoirs written by political and military leaders about these events, it is clear that the former were hoping to avoid fratricidal bloodshed. The latter also felt strong motivation to find a solution that would permit continuation of the Great War until Russia and her allies could win a decisive victory over the Central Powers. But many of these leaders were not fully aware of both perspectives. Basily well knew the views and feelings of the generals at Headquarters and in the various army commands. He also had access to all reports about the situation in the capital as well as to communications between generals and the Duma leaders. In this unique position, he could perceive both aspects of the crisis.

During the first critical months of 1917, Basily served as director of the Diplomatic Chancellery at Army Headquarters in Mogilev. In this capacity, he performed liaison between the Ministry of Foreign Affairs at Petrograd and the Emperor as commander-in-chief of the Russian armed forces. The foreign affairs of Imperial Russia were decided in principle also by the Emperor. During wartime, foreign policy and military operations had to be integrated. It was Basily's role at Army Headquarters to see to it that such coordination was maintained. In this work, he had ready access to the Tsar as well as to the chief of staff, General Mikhail Alexeev. He also kept in close contact with the Grand Dukes and many of the prominent generals who had influence on the Emperor's decisions.

Basily, a lawyer by education, was the only individual at Army Headquarters competent to provide legal advice for the Emperor or the generals and to draft legal documents. When the generals communicated by direct wire to Alexeev their conclusion that the abdication of Nicholas II in favor of his son might solve the crisis, it was only natural that Basily be entrusted with drafting the document. It had to be more than a mere legal formulation to effect a transfer of imperial power from Tsar to heir apparent. Conditions required transformation of Russia from an autocracy, reaching back over the centuries, into a modern constitutional monarchy. Basily had outstanding qualifications to prepare such a document. As a young man, preparing to complete his studies at the famous Alexander Lycée, he had written his dissertation on Speranskii's abortive plan for a constitution. Furthermore, changes envisaged in the abdication document would revive the spirit of the

October 1905 manifesto. Nicholas II had ignored the latter, much to the dismay of the progressive and liberal, albeit pro-monarchist, majority of the Russian intelligentsia. Basily felt himself very much a member of that majority.

As conceived by General Alexeev and generals commanding army groups in the field, the abdication of Nicholas II in favor of his son and appointment of a wise regent would preserve the monarchy but institute a parliamentary system of government somewhat along British lines. If this could not be attained—with the sound of machine gun fire in the streets of Petrograd, with executive power of the cabinet rapidly dis-integrating, with civil war threatening the internal structure of Russia—they feared political chaos at home and military de-feat at the front.

At the request of General Alexeev and well aware of these dangers, Basily sought the solitude of his office to draft a docu-ment that he hoped would pave the way for a political re-alignment in Russia. Such an assignment had no precedent in Russian history. When he presented a draft to his superior, General Alexeev altered only a few words in the first para-graph. Fortunately for scholars, Basily kept all his drafts and was able to bring them out of Russia. The originals are now in the Archives of the Hoover Institution, and a facsimile of the last one is included in this volume. They provide definitive answers to recurring questions about the origins of Nicholas II's abdication document.

Basily also included in his memoirs two accounts by A. I. Guchkov, prominent Russian statesman and member of the Duma, concerning the abdication of the Tsar and the refusal of Grand Duke Michael, brother of Nicholas II, to accept the regency. Both texts were written at Basily's request and their originals, too, are among the Basily Papers in the Archives of the Hoover Institution. Unfortunately, these accounts bear no dates. However, it is clear that they were written much later than Guchkov's earlier published accounts, perhaps dur-ing the 1930s after he had read the writings of other partici-pants in the drama of early March 1917.

Finally, the Basily Papers include a copy of a memorandum entitled "On Our Goals in Regard to the Straits," authored by Basily in November 1914 for the Emperor and the government. In preparing this document, Basily was following a tradition established by his grandfather and father, both Russian diplomats, who had published numerous books and articles on Tsarist vital interests in the Turkish Straits and Constantinople. Naturally, this memorandum was originally produced as a classified paper. Only after the Bolsheviks had come to power was it released for publication in Russian. The Germans found the document interesting as well, and in 1930 it appeared in German translation. In this volume it is being published for the first time in English, as an appendix.

Indeed the time seems propitious for publication of this volume. Thanks to the recent appearance of several new books on the subject, there has been a considerable revival of general interest in the last years of Imperial Russia and the great drama of the ill-starred Romanovs. The memoirs of Nicolas de Basily should be a welcome addition to the documentation of these events and will also add much to the general reader's understanding of conditions that led to the historic events of March 1917. For here is an authoritative eyewitness account of a man who loved Imperial Russia and yet recognized her weakness, who was most loyal to her last ruler, who had the opportunity to observe at first hand her final struggle from a privileged position close to the Emperor, and who moreover possessed the foresight to record it all, with remarkable objectivity, for posterity.

Scholars and general readers alike will be indebted to Nicolas de Basily for having preserved these documents and written these recollections.

W. GLENN CAMPBELL
Director, Hoover Institution

Stanford, California, February 1973

Photographs

Basily as a child.

Basily as a student at the Alexander Lycée.

Tsar Nicholas II and Tsarevich Alexei
in the uniform of the Guard Cossacks,
March 1915.

Sergei D. Sazonov, 1916.

Mikhail V. Alexeev, 1917.

Personnel of the Diplomatic Chancellery at the Imperial Army Headquarters (Stavka), Mogilev, 1916. Left to right: Sergei Valuev, First Secretary; Behr (first name unknown), Vice Director; Nicolas de Basily, Director; Konstantin A. Karasev, a legal adviser not permanently attached to the staff; and Alexander Soldatenkov, Second Secretary.

Nicolas de Basily

Memoirs

Childhood and Adolescence

By my family traditions, my education, and my ties to the West, I belonged to liberal Russian youth.

My family, of foreign origin, owed its salvation to Russia. We came of Albanian feudal leaders from the town of Argirocastro, in Christian Albania. Faithful to their Orthodox beliefs, my ancestors fought the Turks for generations. Russia endeavored to protect the Christians. When one of my ancestors, a Phanariot dignitary devoted to the cause of Greek emancipation, provoked the anger of the Sultan and was condemned to death, it was the Russian ambassador Count Grigorii Stroganov who saved his life by helping him to escape just a few hours before his scheduled execution. The ambassador also helped his wife and children to join him in Russia. His descendants served Russia as diplomats, from father to son, for three generations.

Therefore my father and my grandfather spent much time outside Russia, and married foreigners. My grandfather Konstantin married the granddaughter of Prince Alexander Hanjeri, the hospodar—reigning prince—of Moldavia, who took refuge in Moscow when pursued by Turks. My father, Alexander, married the daughter of Nicholas Callimaki-Catargi, the Rumanian minister of foreign affairs from 1869 to 1871. He was a descendant of the Callimaki princes, who had always been drawn to Western culture. His wife was French, the daughter of Charles Richardot, an officer of the old regime

3

who had rallied to Bonaparte and taken part in the Italian and Egyptian campaigns. The mother of this French officer, née Niem, brought Flemish blood into the family.

Konstantin, my paternal grandfather, was one of the Russian diplomats at the Congress of Paris in 1856. Thereafter he represented Russia on the European commission that prepared the unification of the principalities of Moldavia and Wallachia into what was later to become the Kingdom of Rumania. He had been a schoolboy friend of the famous Russian writer Nikolai Gogol, with whom he later kept up a long correspondence. He was himself attached to the world of belles-lettres, and had ties with Russian literary circles in the first half and the middle of the nineteenth century.

At that time cultivated Russians were divided in a struggle between Slavophiles and Westerners. For the Slavophiles, the civilization of Europe was threatened by decadence. They believed that Russia must follow its own evolution outside the influence of the Western world by rejecting the examples of the West; thus Russia could accomplish its mission of morally regenerating the world. The Westerners correctly imputed the backward condition of the country to the Tatar yoke that had subjected Russia to Asiatic domination for two and a half centuries. They admired the reforms of Peter the Great and his efforts to bring Russia into the heart of Europe. Their goal was to accelerate Russian adoption of all modes of Western life.

While he did not deny Russia's unique aspects, my grandfather leaned toward the Westerners. This was the sense in which he directed his writings. While far from being radical, he hoped to see the reactionary and authoritarian absolutism of Nicholas I (1825–1855) give way to an enlightened monarchy that of its own accord would grant the reforms so long overdue. He therefore became a fervent admirer of the efforts undertaken in this direction by Alexander II (1855–1881). . . .

My grandfather's admiration for Alexander II's reforms led

him to leave the diplomatic corps and settle in the south of Russia, where he had some property, to devote himself to the new elective institutions. He brought into my family a profound veneration for this great Tsar. My father spoke to me of Alexander II with moving affection. While he was still a young diplomat, he had several opportunities to accompany his superiors when they were invited to the Livadia Palace in the Crimea, where the Emperor often passed the winter. My father had occasion to appreciate the charm this benevolent and sociable sovereign exercised over all who approached him, persons who in turn expressed their devotion by embracing him on the shoulder.

Like my grandfather, my father was convinced of the need for a monarchical regime in Russia. As long as the masses remained ignorant, Russia could not do without a strong power. The dynastic tie was equally indispensable, in order to maintain the unity of an empire so immense and heterogeneous it had taken generations of princes a thousand years to forge. "Russia must not proceed too quickly in its development," my father would tell me. "The monarchy must instead take the lead in effecting progress and must fit its methods to the demands of the moment. The weak point of our country is, and has always been, the deep gulf that separates the thin layer of the wealthy, educated, and often highly cultured elite, from the immense mass of the people, most of whom are poor and uneducated. The most urgent task is to provide primary education and vocational training."

The reactionary methods that returned during the reign of Alexander III (1881–1894) did not please my father. He told me then that in these conditions our family should abstain from internal politics and continue to serve the state in the sphere of foreign relations, where we would not be troubled by conflicts of conscience. My father, like my grandfather, was imbued with a sense of duty toward the country: "If our wealth frees us from material concerns, it imposes upon us the obligation to put our power and our knowledge at the service of

our country." This need to justify social advantage by devotion to public affairs was widespread in certain circles of the
nobility. Russian letters, for example Turgenev's novels, give
many examples of "repentant nobles." This state of mind ex-
plains why it was usually members of the nobility who were
at the root of Russian revolutionary movements.

I was born in Paris in 1883. My mother, Eva Callimaki-
Catargi, was a highly cultivated woman of great beauty. As a
young girl, she had lived in London and then Paris, where
her father was the Rumanian minister. Ignace H. J. T. Fantin-
Latour, who taught her painting, did two magnificent portraits
of her.* She is the author of a beautiful volume on Jean Baptiste Isabey, the French miniaturist. Unfortunately, my par-
ents did not get along well and were divorced after a few
years of marriage. During my entire adolescence I lived alone
with my father. He was a kind, fair-minded, generous man of
great intelligence. An art lover, he introduced me to the principal museums of Europe and taught me to appreciate them
while I was still a young child. He would often keep me with
him when he received his friends, who were generally persons
of great culture, and I learned much from their conversations.

When I was ten my father gave me a tutor, a well-educated
young man, Christian Orthodox but of Jewish origin, named
Vladimir Hessen, who lived with us almost three years while
he studied to become a professor. Later he was famous at the
University of St. Petersburg** and was one of the founders of
the Constitutional Democrat or "Cadet" (K.D.) party. Unfortunately he died young. With his great intelligence, his

* One of these paintings, "The Drawing Lesson," is now in the
Modern Museum at Brussels; the other, "The Lady in Gray," is in the
Kroller-Mueller Museum in Otterlo near Amsterdam, a branch of the
Amsterdam Rijksmuseum.
** The name of St. Petersburg, capital of Imperial Russia, was changed
to Petrograd in 1914. Under the Soviet regime this city was renamed
Leningrad and Moscow became the capital.

vast culture, and his thoroughness, his integrity, and his kindness, he might have done great service to the country. I was very fond of him. During our long walks he would talk to me of the sciences, of the history of mankind, of the institutions of various countries, and of the great literary works. He did all this in such an interesting manner that I listened with enchantment. Thus I had no difficulty in assimilating all the knowledge that made up my basic instruction. Both my father and Hessen tried to inculcate in me broad liberal and humanitarian views, and both gave me a taste for learning and work. When I undertook my secondary and university education, I could not imagine being anything but first in my class.

My father's diplomatic career took us first to Constantinople, then to Vienna, and finally to Budapest. When I was fourteen, however, my father felt it was time for me to learn more about my own country. He wanted me to finish my education in Russia; accordingly, he asked to be transferred to the Ministry of Foreign Affairs in St. Petersburg. He became one of the principal advisers of Count Mikhail N. Muraviev, and later of his successor Count Vladimir N. Lamsdorf, the foreign ministers of the period. At first my father was director of the First Section of the ministry—the Balkans and Asia section—and then he became first counselor, holding the rank of undersecretary of state. He also had the responsibilities of Chamberlain of the Court of the Emperor.

We had just settled in St. Petersburg in 1897 when my father came into my room one evening and confided to me that the Russian fleet was going to occupy the Chinese port of Port Arthur.* He did not hide his uneasiness at seeing Russia involved in such a distant region, and said, shaking his head, "Let's hope that this decision doesn't get us into serious

* Russia thus imitated Germany, which had just taken possession of another Chinese port, Kiaochow. Russia's need to have a year-round port on the Pacific dictated this action, since Vladivostok was closed by ice in the winter.

trouble." He did not live to see the Russo-Japanese War, and
was therefore unable to see how accurate had been his pre-
monition.

My father had me enrolled in the Imperial Alexander Lycée,
an institution that offered secondary education courses and
university-level instruction equivalent to the law faculty.*
Latin, French, German, and English were taught there. Knowledge of foreign languages enabled me to finish my courses in
law and political economy with the aid of texts used by students at universities in Paris, Heidelberg, and Oxford. The
function of the Lycée was to prepare the sons of noblemen
for careers in the service of the state. Alexander I had founded
it in 1811. The great poet Alexander Pushkin, one of its first
students, was its shining light. The memorabilia of this genius
were preserved in the Pushkin Museum, which was part of
the Lycée. We dressed in the same uniform worn during his
period: a dark green frock coat with a row of gold buttons
and a red collar with gold braid, and a black three-cornered
hat. The senior class students wore swords which had been
passed from class to class. I received the sword of Wilhelm K.
Kuechelbecker, a friend of Pushkin who took part in the
Decembrist plot against Nicholas I. We piously preserved this
relic in spite of the odor of revolution attached to it. Our
Lycée life was rich in strong traditions. We were proud of our
motto "For the good of all." This precept was not hollow
verbiage: a number of upright and devoted servants of the
state came from the Alexander Lycée during its hundred years
of existence. Among those of my generation were men of
such high ethical values as Vladimir N. Kokovtsov, Sergei D.
Sazonov, Anatolii A. Neratov, Petr M. Kaufman-Turkestanski,
etc.**

* The law school at Russian universities was called "faculty of law."
** Kokovtsov later became minister of finance and prime minister,
Sazonov minister of foreign affairs, Neratov vice minister of foreign
affairs, Kaufman-Turkestanski minister of public education. (Editor's
note.)

There were slightly more than thirty in our class. Among my friends there were many sons of impoverished nobles. Toward the end of the nineteenth century a significant portion of the nobility got by on meager resources while the industrial and commercial class, as elsewhere, became wealthy. The noble origin of the students necessarily determined their political sympathies. All were monarchists, and nearly all were of conservative leaning. Our courses, however, did not incline us toward reaction. On the contrary, they usually had a certain liberal air to them, not what one would expect in an institution intended for the nobility. Our teachers were like the university professors. Most did not hide their personal attachment for liberal, or even socialist, ideas. Sergei A. Muromtsev, our civil law professor, became president of the First Duma.* When the government dissolved that body in 1906 for being too radical, Muromtsev signed the strongly worded protest that became known as the Manifesto of Viborg. Kareev, a member of the K.D. party, taught us about the development of democracy in Western Europe and the United States. Miakotin, who gave remarkable courses in Russian history, was reputed to be a member of the Socialist Revolutionary Party. Iarotskii, a Marxist, taught us political economy. It was only by reading outside of his course that I was able to appreciate other economic doctrines at face value.

The thesis I submitted before leaving the Lycée exemplified the reigning spirit of the institution. I chose for my topic the reforms of Mikhail M. Speranskii, the minister of state under Alexander I who wanted to establish a constitutional regime in Russia. I tried to show that Speranskii was influenced by the many French constitutions of the Revolutionary period. I did not attempt to criticize the limitation of monarchical power; I merely pointed out that such a reform was premature for the beginning of the nineteenth century, where serfdom still existed in Russia. My subject, and the clearly liberal tone of my dis-

* The name Duma was given to the legislative assemblies elected from 1905 until the revolution of 1917.

sertation, did not keep the council from conferring on me its highest award, the Pushkin Medal, in spite of the fact that we were still living under an autocratic regime.*

Nothing could shake the loyalty of the students toward their Emperor. Nicholas II visited the Lycée nearly every winter. He would come unannounced and unattended—he would not even bring an aide-de-camp—and would wear a simple colonel's uniform. Often the Empress would be with him. He went from class to class, stopping to exchange a few pleasant words. We would all follow him to the door with cheers and good wishes. In their enthusiasm, some students would run after his carriage and catch hold of it as the Tsar slowed his team.

The students were united by a solid esprit de corps. Their camaraderie extended beyond members of their individual classes to encompass all who had ever studied at the school. They so supported one another that they were sometimes accused of being a kind of clique. According to one custom, which Pushkin memorialized in some excellent lines of verse, the students and graduates of the Lycée would gather at their alma mater each year on November 1, the anniversary of its founding.** I have the fondest memories of this excellent school, as have my classmates.

If I had gone to the university instead of to the Alexander Lycée, I would have found myself in a completely different atmosphere. The universities, as well as the graduate technical schools in Russia, had large student bodies from all levels of society, with a sizable representation of young people of humble origin who had to work part time to pay for their studies. In other countries and in more recent times, these youths would have expended their excess energy in sporting activities. But

* A copy of the typewritten and multigraphed thesis *Plany gosudarstvennykh preobrazovanii Speranskago* (Speranskii's Plans for Reorganization of the State) is in the Basily Archive in the Hoover Institution. (Editor's note.)
** Or, according to the old Russian style, October 19, a date often commemorated in Pushkin's works.

Russian intellectuals at that time scorned physical exercise, viewing it as a waste of time and beneath the dignity of an educated man. Moreover, the students had no opportunity to form clubs or associations, which were not permitted. Needing some outlet for their gregarious instincts and finding none other available, the students turned to political agitation. Their youthful generosity and inexperience led them naturally to radical ideas. A number of students, especially those among the lowest economic ranks, embraced socialist doctrines. Among the professors, all political ideas were represented, but most professors were liberal or sometimes farther to the left. During the two decades that preceded the revolution, universities became regular breeding grounds for political activities and student strikes took on an endemic character.

I was still a student at the Imperial Alexander Lycée when my father took me with him, in 1899, to the first peace conference at The Hague, where he participated as one of the three Russian plenipotentiaries. This diplomatic assembly, convoked on the initiative of Nicholas II, resulted from a suggestion made by my father to the Tsar. My father had participated in the Russo-Turkish war in 1877–1878. He had come away from it with a vivid horror of war, and he never ceased thinking of ways to avoid it. When he was attending an international parliamentary meeting in the last decade of the nineteenth century at Budapest, where he was consul general, he talked about this subject with several persons and more particularly with a Hungarian friend, Count Albert Apponyi, who took a deep interest in his ideas and offered his support.

The first Hague conference took place in the magnificent Huisten-Bosch room surrounded by the splendid canvases of Jacob Jordaens. Still a very young man, I was discreetly relegated to a corner of the room whence I observed a number of these meetings. Baron Alexander A. de Stal, the Russian ambassador in London, presided over the conference. In his youth he had been a friend of my grandfather. He wore long gray sideburns and was the perfect model of the old-school diplomat. His sharp mind went well with his exquisite courtesy and constant good humor. Fluent in French, he rarely used Russian.

The Russian circular message which had convoked the conference had indicated two objectives: arms limitation, and peaceful settlement of international conflicts. Concerning arms limitations, Russia proposed that all governments commit themselves not to increase their armed forces or their military credits for a fixed period of time, and asked for consideration of means to reduce troop levels and defense budgets in the future. These ideas found warm support on the part of France, represented by Emile Bourgeois, but were firmly rejected by the German delegation and unfortunately were not acted upon. The Russian delegation, feeling that the best way of solving international conflicts was through arbitration, proposed to establish a system for this purpose and sought to make arbitration compulsory for certain specified types of conflict. France and the United States supported this project, but Germany would not hear of compulsory arbitration. Consequently, the conference texts created a system of only voluntary arbitration. To facilitate recourse to this procedure, the conference created a Permanent Court of Arbitration with its seat at The Hague.

In addition to the convention relative to resolution of international conflicts, the conference led to the signature of two other conventions concerning the conduct of war on land and sea. If the achievement of the conference was more modest than one might have hoped, it was because of the objections of the Kaiser's government. He showed clearly, from this date, that he wanted neither to limit his military power in the slightest nor to renounce in any manner his freedom to use force. My father was profoundly disappointed. I witnessed the collapse of a generous initiative that might have enabled us to avoid the terrible dramas which were to unfold before my eyes in years to come.

In 1902, when I was nineteen years old and still at the

Alexander Lycée, fate struck its first blow against me. Almost every year my father and I went to pass a part of our vacation in Paris. This was the year of the first serious epidemic of Spanish influenza. My father was stricken with a violent case of this disease. Frightened, I ran to ask the help of the Russian ambassador, Prince Sergei L. Urusov. He suggested that I see Professor Georges Dieulafoy, one of the great figures in French medicine, who was known all over the world for the brilliance of his courses. His vast clientele included some of the most illustrious men of the era. I rushed to his residence, a magnificent mansion on one of the broad avenues leading to the Arc de Triomphe. Valets in livery—breeches and silk stockings—were stationed at each turn of a vast stairway. After following my guide through luxurious salons filled with art objects, I had a prolonged wait in a beautiful room crowded with other persons. When I finally was ushered into a large office, the professor's secretary received me and fixed the day and hour of the doctor's visit.

On the appointed day, he entered our apartment, a large, handsome man in a frock coat and a high hat. When I asked him to consult with the attending physician, Dr. Dieulafoy refused, adding, "I will see for myself." He started to mount the stairs that led to my father's room. With his hat still on his head, he stopped suddenly and said to me: "It will cost 500 francs" (which at that time was equivalent to 100 dollars in gold). Not having that amount on my person, I ran to procure it. When I returned, I found the famous professor still standing on the steps. After taking my money, he examined my father for a few minutes and then left the sickroom. The consulting physician and I started to ask him some relevant questions when he cut short his visit with the words, "I have nothing to say," and climbed into his carriage. I was furious. Later I learned that Dieulafoy considered the case hopeless and simply did not want his name associated with it.

I went to the ambassador again, and he gave me the address of Professor Louis Landouzy, the other luminary of French

medicine. I went there immediately. I went upstairs in an old
building on the rue de l'Université and rang at the door of
a modest apartment. A short man with a gray goatee opened
the door. He took one look at my anguished appearance and
said, "I shall go to your lodgings immediately." I had scarcely
returned to my father when Professor Landouzy appeared.
He minutely examined the patient and then talked at length
with the attending physician, giving him advice. The professor did not attempt to hide the extreme seriousness of the case
and offered to return if needed. My father died soon afterward.
When I returned to the professor's office to learn how much
I owed him, he charged me a modest amount and, aware of
my distress, endeavored to console me. How right my father
was when he taught me to appreciate the qualities of the heart
in a man much more than those of the mind!

It was a great misfortune for me to lose my father, who
was always so full of affection and care. He had been everything to me, and now I found myself quite alone in St. Petersburg.

Faced with the responsibility of my inheritance, I came to
know what life in the countryside was like. My family's holdings were in Kherson province, in the south of Russia. Ever
since we had been entrusted with service to the state, we had
been unable to care for these holdings directly, which was
the case of many nobles. Such absenteeism obviously did little
to convince the peasantry of the rights of the nobility to their
domains.

For three generations, our holdings had been farmed by
German settlers of Mennonite faith whose ancestors had come
to Russia at the end of the eighteenth century. They still spoke
an old German dialect, Plattdeutsch. They raised mostly wheat
on our land, which we rented to them for a modest fee on the
conditions that they not wear out the soil and that they plant
trees around the villages they established on our land. We
never had trouble with these worthy souls. As the value of the
land and the crops increased with time, we had meetings every

few years with the farmers' delegates and in an amicable spirit
we would determine new rent settlements together. The pro-
ceedings took place in the presence of their spiritual leader,
which in the eyes of the Mennonites excluded any possibility
of dispute by either party to the discussion. We followed the
same practice in case of a bad year, and by common accord
payments were deferred until some more favorable time. These
settlers were excellent workers. They used their savings and
bank loans to buy land, so that by 1914 they were owners of
much of the land around my estate. During the first years of
bolshevism, when I was abroad, they got through to me some
letters saying how much they had regretted to see our good
relations interrupted and how happy they had been before.
Then their letters ceased, and I later learned that all these good
men had been killed by the Soviets under the pretext that they
were exploiters of the peasants—kulaks!

Our relations with our tenant farmers apparently were somewhat exceptional. When I visited the lands of my friends and
those of my father's sister, Princess Euphrosine Urusov, I saw
what conditions prevailed in more typical rural settings of
the early twentieth century.

The great Russian writers have portrayed the paternalistic
relations that once existed between nobles and peasants, but
this type of relationship evidently did not suit our times, and
the younger generations no longer followed it. Nevertheless, I
knew some servants of an extraordinary devotion and some
masters who treated their help like members of the family.

I saw with my own eyes one example of such a paternalistic
tie. An old servant named Kiril, who had worked for my
father and my grandfather, came into my retinue. He was
over eighty. Small and thick-set, he was still remarkably strong
and boasted a mane of black hair. Naturally, we did not give
him much to do, but he had an eye on everything and was
really the master of the house. When I offered him a straight
wage, he grew indignant and protested, "Why do you want to
introduce such a new thing? Do you not always give me money

and clothing when I need it?" One freezing day in winter he came to me and said, "I really should not go out in weather like this. It would also be convenient if you would hire a young woman whom I could guarantee for you as kitchen help." I pretended not to understand his intentions and arranged to hire the young person. When I bought an Oldsmobile in 1903—one of the first automobiles imported into Russia—the faithful Kiril was very critical. "Would your father or grandfather have accepted the idea of using a carriage without horses?" he asked. This time I had to ignore him, but it was not without difficulty. The good old soul never could become accustomed to modern life. One day he was run over by an electric tramcar; the kitchen maid wept copiously.

A few months after my father's death, I found myself the defendant in a court action. My grandfather Konstantin had had some land in the province of Podolia, not far from the Rumanian border, which was in part farmed for him by a little Jewish farmer named Kligman. It had been a long time since this land had been sold by my grandfather. The sons of Kligman were now claiming that my grandfather had owed Kligman a debt. In support of their claim they presented a document dated nearly thirty years earlier, supposedly written and signed by my grandfather. This document was drawn up in such a manner that the high rate of interest over the long period of time, in addition to the penalties stipulated for default of payment, amounted to a sum of such magnitude that it surpassed the total of my wealth, great as it was. Fortunately for me, I was in possession of a large quantity of papers written in my grandfather's hand. When I studied them I concluded beyond doubt that this document, which had appeared out of thin air, was the work of forgers. I then thought it would be worthwhile to see what I could find out about criminal elements in the region who might have been mixed up in this affair. After receiving letters of introduction from the authorities in St. Petersburg, I went to Podolia and asked the local police to aid my investigation. But as soon as the police chief

discovered that the case was still before the courts, he absolutely refused to assist me. The police would favor neither
party in a controversy at the expense of the other. I could
only acquiesce before such scruples and decided, in the naiveté
of my youth, to play the detective myself. This adventure
nearly cost me dearly. During a night spent alone in a modest
inn lost in the countryside, I had to fight off a murder attempt
with my revolver.

My adversaries won the first trial and the first appeal. It
was only after six years of inquiry and further appeals that I
was able to assemble irrefutable proof of forgery, which
brought me victory before the Senate, sitting as the Supreme
Court. Vasilii A. Maklakov, who later became the greatest
orator in the Duma, was my lawyer. This marked the beginning of my friendship with this perfect man and great patriot.

This incident would not bear retelling except for the overly
harsh opinions that prevail concerning administration of justice in Russia during the old regime. In this case, the situations
of the parties were quite unequal: two obscure Jewish rustics
on one side, on the other a family well known in the capital of
the Empire and in court circles. Nevertheless, the police, always under attack, never swerved from the strictest impar-
tiality. Tsarist Russia had come a long way from the days
when the arbitrary dominated the legal.

— 2 —

The Making of a Diplomat

In May 1903 I finished my university courses at the Alexander Lycée and went into the Ministry of Foreign Affairs. I passed the diplomatic examination immediately and was assigned to the Chancellery of the ministry. This division of the central administration of the ministry dealt with political questions relative to Europe (except the Balkan states) and America, while the Balkans and Asia came under the First Section of the ministry. The Chancellery functioned as the minister's cabinet and also handled his confidential correspondence and coding. Young attachés began their apprenticeship coding and decoding secret telegrams, a task that went on day and night through changing shifts. This work was done by a small and carefully chosen group, to assure the necessary secrecy.

I had just entered the foreign service when, in June 1903, I was sent to Vienna and Rome as courier in charge of the diplomatic pouch to our representatives in these capitals. In Rome I called on Gubastov, our minister to the Vatican, who had been a friend and colleague of my father. It happened that one of the documents I brought him dealt with a subject of special interest to Pope Leo XIII: the conditions of Catholic worship in the Russian Empire. Gubastov had requested an audience to converse with the Holy Father and proposed that I accompany him, saying, "I would be happy to give you the opportunity to meet one of the greatest personages of our

18

time. You who are still so young will one day regard this as one of the most interesting memories of your lifetime. You will have seen the man who has given to the papacy a prestige unknown since medieval times." More than half a century has gone by since then, and I highly appreciate having had the honor of knowing this great humanist.

Leo XIII received us in a small room. An old man of eighty-three, dressed in white, he was seated in a large armchair. He seemed very frail; his face was gaunt and yet his eyes burned with energy. He so resembled Houdon's famous statue of Voltaire in the Comédie Française that I had the impression of having seen him before. However, the similarity of features did not hide the difference of expression: here, instead of the malice of the French writer, there was great gentleness and benevolent animation. The Pope talked first with Gubastov and then, after my presence had been explained to him, had me sit next to him on a little stool and explained to me his views about diplomacy.

A good diplomat must of course serve his country loyally, he began, but faithfulness to this duty must never allow him to forget the higher interests of humanity. The best way to serve these was to work endlessly for understanding between nations and for the maintenance of peace. As I listened to the words of this holy man, I thought of my father, who had been inspired by the same precepts when he had the idea of an international accord to eliminate recourse to war, and when he prepared the 1899 peace conference.

I had just returned to Russia when the telegraph announced the news of the death of Leo XIII after a papacy of twenty-five years.

At that time, Count Vladimir Lamsdorf was at the head of the Ministry of Foreign Affairs.* He was an honest, conscientious, and competent civil servant who had spent his entire career in the central offices of the ministry, but he lacked breadth. According to the traditions of Russian autocracy,

* From 1900 to 1906.

foreign affairs as well as military administration were the
private reserve of the monarch. So Count Lamsdorf considered
himself more as a man to carry out his sovereign's wishes than
as a counselor responsible for his own decisions. During Lamsdorf's tenure, A. M. Bezobrazov, an officer of the guard,
abused the confidence of Emperor Nicholas in procuring assistance from authorities in the Far East for a group of Russian speculators who wanted concessions for forest exploitation
in northern Korea. The Japanese, who were already upset by
the growing activities of Russia in Manchuria, felt obliged
to put an end to this latest advance. Neither the leaders nor
the public properly estimated the true power of the Japanese
forces, while at the same time most of them overestimated
Russia's capabilities in an area so far removed from its center.
Sergei Witte, the great finance minister, did not share these
dangerous illusions and used all his power to prevent a conflict; but a foolhardy clique led by Bezobrazov, by Admiral Evgenii Alexeev, the governor-general of the Russian provinces
in the Far East, and by Viacheslav K. von Plehve, the minister of the interior, got the upper hand. On February 4, 1904,
the Japanese fleet attacked the Russian bastion at Port Arthur
without warning, thus foreshadowing Japanese action thirty-
seven years later at Pearl Harbor. Count Lamsdorf had been
against the Korean adventure that touched off the conflict,
but he did not have enough character to give Witte the resolute support he needed to turn the Tsar away from a war that
was to be so damaging to the prestige of Russia and the
imperial regime.

Witte had for years maintained close relations with my
father, and after my father's death Witte and his wife very
graciously and simply took me into their close circle. I was
particularly friendly with their charming daughter Vera, who
later married Cyril Naryshkin. Thus I had many opportunities to hear Witte express himself openly. He was a tall, well-
built man given to heavy gestures. He had a high brow and a
blunt nose, and wore a little chestnut beard streaked with

gray. From 1893 to 1903 he had been head of the Ministry of Finance of the Empire and had accomplished much during his tenure. In order to balance the budget and at the same time reduce the toll of alcoholism in the country, Witte had established a state monopoly for the sale of alcoholic beverages.* He had been able to halt the depreciation of the Russian monetary unit, the ruble, by taking adroit financial steps, and had stabilized it by placing Russia on the gold standard. Having thus reestablished confidence in the ruble, he had applied himself to attracting much-needed foreign capital to accelerate Russia's economic growth. The government had arranged a sizable loan in France, and then other countries followed suit.

Witte also greatly expanded the railroad system and gave strong impetus to the development of industries by establishing relatively modest customs rates. During the ten years of his wise financial management the income of the treasury doubled.

While he wanted to see foreign capital employed in Russia, Witte was fundamentally opposed to foreign control over any any sector of the economy. He was not overly concerned about such an eventuality, however: he was convinced that by means of sound policies Russia could progress rapidly enough that domestic capital would soon replace that from abroad. His predictions were largely justified during the period from 1905 to 1914, which was marked by an enormous economic growth owing to his initiatives.

But his ambitious and domineering personality and his rude

* The liquor monopoly provoked much criticism of Witte. He was reproached for basing state income on the people's penchant for drink. It is true that this monopoly produced more than a quarter of the state revenues. Defenders of the monopoly held that it attenuated the evils of alcoholism by restricting impure products. Moreover, the annual per capita consumption of alcohol was lower in Russia than in France, England, Germany, and some other European countries. The *muzhik* [Russian peasant] did not harm himself so much because he drank a lot as because he drank irregularly and at times greatly overindulged.

manners finally alienated the Emperor and created many en-
mities in governmental circles. In 1903 he was removed from
his position as minister of finance. Witte had owed his career
to Alexander III. He was attached to that Tsar's memory and
was quick to praise his firm character, his consistency, and
his clear and simple conduct. Though Witte did not criticize
Alexander's successor, one felt he was wearied by the weakness and instability of Nicholas II.

My work in the Ministry of Foreign Affairs allowed me
enough free time to finish my law studies and to have some
social life, which gave me a chance to ease the loneliness that
had weighed on me since my father's death. I had the good for-
tune to have several friends who invited me out often. I was
still timid and gauche, however, and in course of my first social
ventures I committed many lamentable blunders.

On one occasion I received an invitation from Prince
Abamelik Lazarev and his wife Maria, née Demidov. I knew
that they had liked my father, but I had not yet met them. At
lunch time I presented myself at their lovely home on Nevsky
Prospect, the main thoroughfare of the capital, and was shown
into a small drawing room. After a brief wait, the master of
the house came and found me and questioned me in a friendly
fashion about my activities. Time passed and I was beginning
to feel ill at ease, when my host asked if I would care for
some refreshment. I stammered a few words. He disappeared,
then returned to lead me to a vast Empire-style dining hall.
There was a single place setting on the large table. Prince
Abamelik offered me a seat, took a chair next to mine, and
gave me an excellent meal. Then he told me, "Don't forget
that we're counting on you for dinner." I had come for lunch,
although I had been invited for dinner! When I returned, in
evening dress, several hours later, I found about twenty persons
in the salons. The beautiful young mistress of the house, a
slender brunette with magnificent eyes, managed to dispel my
intense embarrassment with her kindness and her spontaneous
laughter.

Not long afterward, I was invited to a large party given by the ambassador of Italy. Intimidated by the importance of the crowd, I had taken refuge near a column when my attention was arrested by the sound of tearing cloth. I looked, and there beneath my feet was a magnificent piece of red velvet, which could only have been the train of a sumptuous dress. In consternation, I raised my eyes. Before me stood an unknown and thoroughly irate lady. She was a very beautiful brunette with superb shoulders and slightly olive tint to her complexion. Suddenly her expression mellowed. She took my hand, and with a charming smile said, "Do not be so upset. It is nothing at all." This compassionate lady was one of the most attractive ladies in St. Petersburg. Several years later she was married in a morganatic ceremony to the Grand Duke Paul, the Emperor's uncle, and was given the title of Princess Paley. She never reproached me for my inexcusable clumsiness, and I have always been grateful to her for the grace she showed to a confused and unhappy young man.

Social life as it existed in Russia before the fall of the monarchy offered a particular attraction. Many foreigners who lived then in St. Petersburg or Moscow have spoken of its charm. The pleasantness of life was due to the simplicity of human relationships, to the natural generosity of the people and to their great hospitality. These traits characterized every level of society. Everyone took pleasure in receiving guests and each did so as his means permitted. If receptions in the homes of the wealthy were often sumptuous and sparkling, those of more modest means were not in the least embarrassed at sharing with more affluent guests the little they could offer. No one attached much importance to the luxury or modesty of the setting, the refinement or simplicity of the fare. Often friends would drop in without an invitation and take pot luck. Their hosts would simply add a place setting and offer whatever there was by reducing portions all around. At about ten in the evening, the lady of the house would put a samovar in the dining room and friends would come for a cup of tea after the theater, without having to call first. This was known as coming to the call of the "little light" (*na ogoniok*); in other words, one would come in upon seeing a light in the window.

Russians are known for their love of conversation. They expound on all kinds of topics, some of them entirely abstract. As one popular expression put it, "Does God exist or not?" These gatherings would often run late into the night. People willingly welcomed the friends of their friends. Foreigners likewise were readily received into the local families. In the countryside, the hospitality was even greater. Princess Euphrosine Urusov, my aunt, often set her table for thirty or forty persons, and she had even added an extra house to lodge her guests. Persons in difficulty, sometimes even people she hardly knew, would appear at her home in the summer and stay a month or more. Such hospitality was one of the accepted modes of charity, and Russian novels give vivid examples of men or women who lived off the hospitality of others. Music also played an important role in life. Whenever several young men or women got together they played the piano and sang.

The generally friendly attitude of the people did not rule out manifestations of completely different feelings. Many of these hospitable persons were readily disposed to criticize. Intrigues and slander campaigns abounded. All human societies suffer from this malady, particularly in elite circles, but it was perhaps more accentuated in St. Petersburg, where almost everyone's energies were absorbed in government service and what was seen as a too rapid promotion could provoke envy and calumny. On the other hand, close friendships formed in the schools, the regiments, and even in the administration were often so strong that they constituted a powerful defense against such maneuvering.

Russian society was still divided into classes. As in all societies where either one's ancestors or one's rank in the state hierarchy counted for more than one's wealth, differences in material conditions did not have much influence on social relationships. Wealthy persons and those without resources mingled freely if they came from the same social category or if they had acceded to it for a good reason. The little circle of the upper nobility was exclusive, accepting persons of lesser origin only when they had achieved the highest of ranks in the state bureaucracy. Dignitaries in the Imperial Court were drawn from this circle or became part of it.

In preceding reigns the sovereigns kept up their relations with the society of the capital, but these contacts diminished considerably under the last two tsars. While Emperor Alexander II had enjoyed wide social contacts, his successors, Alexander III and Nicholas II, were too absorbed by their family lives to look elsewhere for diversion. Empress Alexandra's timidity, and then her poor health, even further removed Nicholas II and his wife from the life of the capital.

In my time there were very few large receptions at the Court, and those only on occasions when they were unavoidable. The beautiful halls of the Winter Palace in St. Petersburg and those of Tsarskoe Selo and Peterhof in the suburbs of the capital no longer knew the festivities of the past. I can remember only one important event that was not of a ceremonial nature at the palace of St. Petersburg. The Grand Duke Konstantin, a cousin of the Emperor and a fine man, was a gifted poet and had done a beautiful translation into Russian verse of Shakespeare's *Hamlet*. He wanted to play the role of the unhappy prince himself. The play was presented before the Emperor and the Court, as well as the literary friends of the Grand Duke, in the fine palace theater known as the "Hermitage." It was a great artistic success.

Of the imperial family, only the Grand Duke Vladimir, the Emperor's uncle, and his wife the Grand Duchess Maria Pavlovna, maintained steady relations with St. Petersburg society. The Grand Duke Vladimir had great bearing. He knew how to assert his rank without losing his pleasant manner. After his death his wife continued to receive a circle of friends,

and the most noteworthy diplomats, in her beautiful palace on
the Neva Quay. She was witty and sophisticated. Empress
Alexandra did not like her, and the royal entourage reproached her for being a schemer. Her oldest son, Cyril
(whom I resembled, according to his father), fell in love
with the English Princess Victoria, daughter of the Duke of
Edinburgh and cousin of Empress Alexandra,* and wanted to
marry her. But this would require the divorce of Princess Victoria, who for some years had been the wife of the Grand Duke
of Hesse, brother of Empress Alexandra. For this reason the
Empress violently opposed the marriage plan. Cyril, brooding
with resentment, went to Sicily. I happened to be there at the
same time, and can attest to his bitterness. The lovers ulti-
mately overcame these obstacles and formed a close union.
Their son Vladimir is presently the legitimate pretender to
the Romanov crown.

The Grand Duke Paul and his morganatic wife, Princess
Paley, frequently were hosts at luncheon or dinner in their
beautiful residence at Tsarskoe Selo when they were not at
their home at Boulogne-sur-Seine in the outskirts of Paris.
The other elder members of the imperial family led a retired
life and saw little of St. Petersburg society. Most of the younger
generation of grand dukes were uninteresting and not well
educated. Several of them discredited themselves by their
intemperate habits. Generally speaking, the princes of the
reigning house did not know how to choose their friends and
were susceptible to flattery. That was what my father meant
when he advised me to avoid too close contact with grand
dukes.

There was one group in the aristocracy that kept away from
the Court. These were chiefly members of the oldest noble
families who held liberal ideas and did not approve of the political tendencies espoused by the last two tsars. They belonged
to such illustrious families as the Dolgorukiis, Trubetskois,
Lvovs, Viazemskiis, Panins, etc.

* They were both granddaughters of Queen Victoria of England.

I will mention only a few of the most important or most pleasant salons of St. Petersburg. The foreign diplomats went often to that of Countess Kleinmichel, an intelligent woman well informed on political affairs. She had two charming daughters, one of whom, Madame Lopukhin, died very young and was widely mourned. The last great social affair before the war of 1914 was a costume ball given by Countess Kleinmichel in her handsome house on Sergeevskii Street. Her guests came dressed in sumptuous costumes of every epoch. Among my paintings was the portrait of a Venetian dignitary of the Renaissance period clad in a robe of crimson silk, and this served as the model for my costume. I have also kept the memory of another beautiful ball, an earlier one given by Countess Elizabeth Shuvalov, née Princess Bariatinskii, in her Fontanka Palace. This charming grande dame was devoted to good works and rendered great service during the war of 1914.

The most attractive private residence in St. Petersburg was that of Prince Felix and Princess Zenaïda Iusupov.* It housed a magnificent collection of paintings. Princess Iusupov was a very beautiful woman whose hair had turned completely white when she was quite young, which enhanced her beauty. Serov, the best of the modern Russian painters, made a magnificent portrait of her. Nicholas, her oldest son, was a charming boy whom I met at my friend Mukhanov's house. No sooner had Nicholas finished his university studies than he fell in love with the wife of an officer of the guard, who challenged him to a duel in which Nicholas was killed. Duelling still was recognized as a means of settling a point of honor although not many duels actually took place. It was wise to be skilled in arms, however, just in case.

The most elegant woman in St. Petersburg was Princess Olga Orlov, née Princess Beloselskii. While not beautiful, she had a lovely figure and a distinguished manner. Her husband,

* The younger son of this couple was Prince Iusupov, also named Felix, who took part in the assassination of Rasputin in 1916.

the fat Prince Vladimir Orlov, was one of the very few personal friends of the Emperor.

Two American ladies had taken St. Petersburg by conquest. They had both married officers of the guard. One, born Whittier, was the wife of Prince Sergei Beloselskii, who succeeded Prince Victor Napoleon Bonaparte as commander of the Lancer Guards. The other, a charming granddaughter of President Ulysses S. Grant, became the wife of Prince Mikhail Cantacuzino, the aide-de-camp of the Grand Duke Nicholas during the war of 1914.

Countess Sofia Panin was especially interested in social questions and had a marked penchant for liberal circles. Princess Viazemskii, born Countess Levashov, was a highly educated and distinguished woman who had the same political leanings. Her son, one of my good childhood friends, became the aide-de-camp of Alexander Guchkov, minister of war in the Provisional Government, and was killed at Guchkov's side by rebel soldiers at the beginning of the revolution in 1917. Alexander Polovtsov and his charming wife held one of the most pleasant salons in St. Petersburg. They lived in a lovely Empire-style residence on The Islands. During the summer I would visit them at their estate near Luga, not far from St. Petersburg. There they had a baroque-style house built around a large and comfortable circular salon. The house overlooked a beautiful lake surrounded by forests. Polovtsov was highly cultured and possessed of a refined artistic sense. He had been brought up among objects of art. His grandfather had assembled a beautiful collection and had given the city of St. Petersburg a fine museum of decorative arts, the Stieglitz Museum. It was my friend Polovtsov and the charming painter Alexander Benois who gave me advice when I began to collect works of the Russian painters of the eighteenth century who are so little known outside of Russia.*

* A collection of the paintings that belonged to Nicolas and Lascelle de Basily, including works by several Russian masters of the eighteenth century as well as paintings by Francesco Guardi, Sir Joshua

The officers of the Imperial Guard, who came from the best families, took an active part in the social life of the capital. These elite troops were stationed in St. Petersburg and its environs. The most dashing regiments were those of the Chevalier Garde and the Horse Guard, in their magnificent white uniforms, armor, and helmets topped with two-headed eagles. Since several of my school friends served in the Horse Guard, I was invited from time to time to be a guest at the regimental mess. Though not without a certain protocol, these dinners were marked by a spirit of genuine cordiality. Each officer would offer the guest a glass of champagne, which he could hardly refuse. Thus the regular participants in the mess were not likely to drink too much, but the guest ran a strong risk of getting quite drunk. I used to try to minimize the effect by drinking a glass of olive oil before going to these dinners.

One of the officers whom I knew at that time was Baron Gustav Mannerheim of the Chevalier Garde, a tall, handsome man of faultless demeanor. I became better acquainted with him during a trip we took together from Paris to St. Petersburg. He struck me as an intelligent man, but one who was cold and insensitive in temperament. He later became a general. After the revolution of 1917 he led the Finnish troops in their victorious battle against the Red Army and was elected president of Finland.

High society in St. Petersburg revolved around the Court, the Guard, and the government, and was completely separated from the world of industry, banking, and commerce. There was still a prejudice against business in Russia. Apart from government service, the nobles continued in their historic tradition as owners and managers of land, or as urban landlords, but they were looked upon with disfavor if they en-

Reynolds, Joseph Vernet, and others, was donated by Mrs. Lascelle de Basily to the Hoover Institution at Stanford University. This collection now adorns the Nicolas de Basily Room at the Institution. (Editor's note.)

gaged in other kinds of remunerative activities. In consequence, the wealthiest persons remained outside the social
world.

The greatest fortunes of Russia belonged to the tradesmen
of Moscow. Among them were commercial fortunes that went
back two or three centuries. Generally speaking, the business
people in Moscow were true to the old traditions. A number
of them were affiliated with the Old Believers, an offshoot of
the Orthodox church which adhered to the old rituals. Others
were open to progress and innovation. These men established
large and powerful industries, like the Morozovs, for example, the great textile manufacturers. There were also some
highly cultured men in their ranks. Some patronized the arts
or were art lovers, like the Tretiakovs, who founded the outstanding gallery of Russian art in Moscow that bears their
name. In the interest of cultural propagation, the Soldatenkovs
founded a publishing house that specialized in the production
of inexpensive editions of many of the works of the best authors. The wealthy businessmen and industrialists of Moscow
further showed great generosity in founding hospitals, schools,
and other charitable institutions of all types.

St. Petersburg was not the only center of intellectual activity
in the country. Moscow was another important center of
thought. Its university enjoyed great prestige; and while the St.
Petersburg press was the best known, that of Moscow was not
without influence. Excellent night trains connected the two
cities, but nevertheless contacts between them were limited.
This was especially true with respect to the essentially different
society circles of the two cities. It was possible to attend St.
Petersburg salons for years without ever meeting a Muscovite.

The capital founded by Peter the Great still fulfilled its
founder's objective as a window on Europe, while Moscow
remained utterly autochthonous, Russian in style. The ancient
metropolis boasted its Kremlin, birthplace of the first tsars, and
its old Byzantine churches. St. Petersburg, in contrast, bore the
indelible mark of the Western Europe of the eighteenth cen-

tury. The center of life in the Empire was along the quays of the Neva, which were lined by sumptuous residences of baroque or Louis XVI style ranging from St. Isaac's cathedral and the Admiralty to the Marble Palace of the Grand Duke Konstantin and the Winter Palace, that immense imperial residence. On the other side of the great river sprawled the ancient fortress of St. Peter and Paul, its granite fortifications dominated by the gilded belfry spire of the sepulchral church of the Russian emperors and their families. The Palace Quay was a favorite spot for strolling during the short winter days when the ice that covered the broad course of the Neva sparkled in the sun. Pedestrians moved side by side with open sleighs that were steered by drivers dressed in the Russian manner, that is to say with caftans padded at the waist to give the driver a pyramidal silhouette. Young people who wanted to appear elegant rode in backless sleighs so narrow that if a couple occupied them, the man would have to hold his lady by the waist to keep her from falling. These light vehicles were swept along over the snow by fast Russian trotting horses. The traditional modes of transportation were gradually replaced by automobiles, and eventually only the *izvozchiki,* the drivers of the light sleighs or rental carriages, remained to preserve the local color. Another picturesque note was added by the wet-nurses who, during fine weather, suckled babies in the gardens of the city. These young women, many of them quite pretty, dressed in the manner of the Russian peasant women of earlier days—small open vests over white shirts and brightly colored full skirts. When the day grew chilly, they would add a *sarafan,* a kind of embroidered tunic. *A kokoshnik,* shaped like a diadem and encrusted with colored stones, served as a cap.

Easter in Russia was the time of the most beautiful religious ceremonies. Evening mass at majestic St. Isaac's cathedral drew multitudes of worshippers, each carrying a lighted candle. Thousands of little flames twinkled softly in the semidarkness of the vast nave. There the crowd gathered

to await the appearance of bishops and priests robed in gold
brocade and coiffed with jeweled mitres. The choir began to
sing the superb Gregorian hymns and the church was filled
with the resonance of their voices. At midnight the clergy left
the church and circled it three times, followed by the crowd.
The evocation of the Resurrection flooded the hearts of the
faithful with hope and joy, and—as was the custom of the
day—men and women would kiss all those about them three
times on the cheek, even if they were strangers, and say,
"Christ is risen!" The others would respond, "Truly, He is
risen."

As in all Nordic countries, the most pleasant season in St.
Petersburg was the time of the midnight sun. As early as
May people took advantage of the light to walk at ten or
eleven o'clock at night in the outskirts of the city, in the
lovely park in the Neva delta commonly called "The Islands."
One could watch the sun sink beneath the horizon and re-
appear almost immediately, and the diaphanous light enhanced
the beauty of gardens intersected by arms of the river. Carriages rolled by one after another, and friends greeted friends.
Pretty courtesans drew admiring glances. If one was disposed
to spend the night in diversion or if in a romantic mood (so
predisposed by the pale light), then he might visit the gypsies
—together with an agreeable companion, if possible—and
hear their voices singing sentimental ballads. One drank and
one wept.

The concert halls and theaters were very popular. Interest
was concentrated particularly on the two composers who so
vigorously expressed the true spirit of the Russian school of
music: Musorgskii—dead for many years—and Rimskii-Korsakov, who taught at the St. Petersburg Conservatory. As for
Chaikovskii, his opera *Eugène Onegin* and his ballets, *Swan
Lake* and *Sleeping Beauty,* had become very popular after his
death, but his concert works were not yet as much appreciated
in Russia as they were to be later. The Russian public had
such an affection for music and song that several operas played

simultaneously in St. Petersburg, and the large cities of the interior, such as Moscow, Odessa, etc., also had permanent opera companies.

The Mariinskii Imperial Theater, financed by the government, was designed for the presentation of opera and ballet. The auditorium was large and stately, decorated with gilt and blue silk draperies. The most popular opera singers of the era were the tenor Figner and his wife Medea, one of the most brilliant Carmens I have ever heard. Figner's best performance was in the role of Lenskii in *Eugène Onegin*. Another excellent tenor, Sobinov, won ardent acclaim for his admirable performance in *Sadko* by Rimskii-Korsakov.

The Italian opera of St. Petersburg drew the best singers in the world. The opera presented regular performances each winter until the war in 1914. Its place in the musical world was later taken by the Metropolitan Opera of New York, which with the support of the wealth and generosity of the United States supplanted and—I must say—eclipsed the earlier Russian triumphs. Artists who had won the heart of the public were the object of warm demonstrations and reaped huge rewards. Frequently the great woman singers, dancers, and players would find expensive jewels in bouquets of flowers offered them, with nothing expected in return. Famous tenors like Masini, Francesco Tamagno, and later Enrico Caruso drew applause every season. The public's favorite was the baritone Matteo Battistini, who was not only a magnificent artist but a highly refined, cultivated man. In order to make it possible for him to sing the part of Werther, Jules Massenet adapted his score to Battistini's baritone. The tenor arias of Anton Rubinstein's *The Demon* and of Chaikovskii's *Onegin* were similarly transposed for him and he achieved formidable success in their rendition. I chanced to meet Battistini toward the end of his long career, in Prague in 1925. He spoke with feeling of his stays in Russia, while I recalled the marvelous hours he had given his Russian friends.

During one season of Italian opera, the *Traviata* cast

brought together Caruso, Battistini—and Lina Cavalieri. This splendid creature, the most beautiful woman I ever saw in my life, first appeared in St. Petersburg around 1900. Still quite young, she had been brought there by a brilliant officer, Prince Anatolii Bariatinskii, who had spirited her away from a wealthy Italian. Since she had posed for sculptors, the art supply stores sold photographs of her that permitted one to admire her, unveiled, from head to toe. I wanted to have an autographed photo. Encouraged by my father, I went to see her with a friend, dressed in my student uniform. She welcomed us gracefully and signed for each of us one of the photographs we had brought. A good Italian, Lina Cavalieri loved music. Accompanied by a chaperone, she often attended performances of the Italian opera, always dressed tastefully in a pale, very low-cut evening gown. So extraordinary was her beauty that many spectators—women as well as men—would remain in the theater during intermission instead of moving to the foyer. They stood before her loge as if frozen, their eyes fixed on this feminine marvel in a way that would normally have been considered rude. Each time she saw *Traviata* she shed bitter tears. Since she had a fine voice, she conceived the ambition of singing the role of Violetta and worked hard until the two most famous singers of the age agreed to appear with her. While she never attained the virtuosity of the great sopanos who had been applauded at St. Petersburg, she put so much feeling into her singing that the audience was greatly moved.

Feodor Chaliapin had just attained fame when I saw him for the first time in the enormous Theater of the People. He played and sang the role of the monk Dosifei in an artistic performance of Musorgskii's *Khovanshchina*. This famous basso was an exceptional actor as well as a singer. In *Boris Godunov* he sang Pushkin's beautiful verses, set to music by Musorgskii, with such art that he forced the audience to share the anguish of this man vanquished by remorse. One evening at my house in St. Petersburg, very gently and without accompaniment he began to sing. He was a giant, simple in manner and a bit unpolished, but richly gifted, as men of humble Russian origin often are.

The ballet, like the imperial opera and theater companies, was supported by the state. Each Sunday the beau monde would meet at the Marinskii Theater for the most beautiful evenings of ballet. The dancers formed a little world apart. From the time they entered the dancing school in St. Petersburg, they were imbued with reverence for the art to which they had dedicated themselves. The atmosphere in which they moved was such that most of the ballerinas lived perfectly respectable, or at least very discreet, lives. Anna Pavlova dominated the entire history of Russian ballet by virtue of the perfection and exaltation of her art. I made her acquaintance at the beginning of her career, when she lived with her mother in a modest apartment behind the Tsarskoe Selo railway station. She spoke to us then of her aspirations. Ever since she had first attended a ballet performance as a small girl, she had been captivated by this vocation. For her, dance was the most beautiful way of externalizing man's inner feelings. If one wanted to serve this art, one had literally to give both body and soul to it. She was prepared to work untiringly, striving constantly for perfection, in ceaseless pursuit of her dream of beauty. She was a true vestal, faithful to the end to her creed.*

Another ballerina, the exquisite Tamara Karsavina, possessed an impeccable technique enhanced by delicate and distinguished grace. In Chaikovskii's *Sleeping Beauty* she was unforgettable. She married a distinguished diplomat, Henry James Bruce, secretary of the British embassy in St. Petersburg during the First World War. Mikhail Fokin was also a dancer of admirable technique and perfect taste. He found his

* As I write these lines, I have in front of me a portrait of Pavlova in the "Death of the Swan" scene. This photograph was inscribed by her to the minister of foreign affairs of Nicholas II, Sazonov, who willed it to me along with his papers. It is a precious memento, both of the great artist and of my esteemed chief.

real vocation as the celebrated choreographer of the Marinskii
Theater. Vaslav Nizhinskii made his appearance in the firma-
ment of great artists only after Sergei Diaghilev, aided by Fokin,
organized the famous foreign tours of the Russian ballet in
1909. The harmony and precision of Nizhinskii's dancing were
heightened by his great athletic strength. He gave the impression of remaining effortlessly suspended in the air. The light-
ness of his great leap in *The Specter of the Rose* seemed to
defy the laws of gravity.

In the first years of the twentieth century Anton Chekhov
and Maxim Gorkii were writing their best theatrical works,
which attracted general attention immediately. The plays of
these two great writers presaged the future of the country. The
first depicted the decline of the nobility, the second, the rise
of the worker. The best playhouse in St. Petersburg was the
Alexandrinskii Imperial Theater, which was subsidized by the
state. It was graced by the performances of Savina, a highly
respected artist, and Komisarzhevskaia. The Moscow Art Theater, a private enterprise, had attained under the driving force
of the great actor and director Stanislavskii a perfection until
then unknown in Russia, and perhaps anywhere else, in the
performance of all its actors and the minute detail of its
scenery. The Little Theater in St. Petersburg centered around
the talented actress Iavorskaia, and was principally devoted
to the performance of foreign plays.

Most educated persons knew French. The upper class used
the language so much that social conversations proceeded
spontaneously in either French or Russian. Moreover the
capital boasted a French theater that was subsidized by the
state. From September till May a troupe of actors recruited
in France presented the latest successful plays from Paris in
the attractive auditorium of the Marinskii Imperial Theater.
Each week they gave a new play, opening on Saturdays before
an elegant audience who, for the most part, knew one another.
I tried not to miss any of these productions, which I always
watched from the same seat in the first row. Andrieux and

Velbel were two long-time regular members of the company, and for a while Lucien Guitry was part of the troupe.

The success of the Russian theater owed in part to the care given to the staging, especially to the costumes and the settings. Here the modern Russian painters Bakst, Alexander Benois, Bilibin, Dobuzhinskii, and Kustodiev made great contributions.

The Russian public were slow to appreciate the plastic arts of their country. The Empress Catherine contributed much to the blossoming of these arts. She created the Academy of Fine Arts in St. Petersburg and collected some magnificent paintings by the best Italian, French, and Dutch painters which formed the core of the Hermitage collection in St. Petersburg * and inspired generations of Russian artists. This great sovereign was able to recognize the talent of such portrait painters as Dmitrii Levitskii, Vladimir Borovikovskii, and Stepan Shchukin. Although their art was inspired by the French and English schools of the eighteenth century, it nevertheless bore its own characteristic stamp. Subsequently forgotten for a while, these three masters came to be appreciated at their real value only at the time of the beautiful Russian art exposition which I was privileged to see in 1902 at the Taurida Palace in St. Petersburg. In the salons of Princess Maria Shakhovskoi I learned to admire another Russian painter of the eighteenth century, Sylvester Shchedrin, whose too rare works include some very beautiful Italian landscapes.

For half a century the Academy of Fine Arts was the center of artistic progress, but, as is often the case, its official curriculum eventually declined into conventional formalism. The choice of canvases admitted for expositions and academic competitions provoked protest, and in 1870 a group of thirteen painters led by Kramskoi, an excellent portraitist, founded the "Itinerants" association, so named because they organized their

* The most beautiful of these paintings were sold by the Soviets and today constitute the principal attraction of the National Gallery in Washington, D.C.

own expositions and moved them from one city to another. Ilia Repin joined this group—a highly talented artist who painted with a powerful hand but was sometimes too easily contented with facile effects. Two painters of quite different nature who were inspired by the past also joined: Viktor Vasnetsov and Surikov. The former devoted himself to religious subjects and attempted to revive the Byzantine style, while the latter, both a realist and a visionary, tried to bring to life some of the dramatic events of Russian history. The "Itinerants" allowed themselves to be too greatly influenced by public opinion. Instead of demanding that painters dedicate themselves to the pure and simple cult of beauty and truth, the public wanted them to apply themselves to contemporary Russian problems, to put their brushes to work for a moral, political, or social ideal, after the manner of writers of the time. This produced a reaction aimed at liberating art from anything foreign to the demands of esthetics, which in turn gave rise to a new movement, formed in 1899 around the review *The World of Art* (*Mir iskusstva*) and led by Diaghilev, a man full of ideas and taste though not himself a painter. From the time of this new group's inception, I followed its expositions each year at the Great Morskaia in St. Petersburg with the greatest interest. There one could see the beautiful Russian landscapes, so lifelike, from the hand of Levitan; the brilliant canvases of Maliavin, who knew how to depict Russian peasant women in all the vigor of life; and finally the majestic works of Serov, whose portraits, such as those of Emperor Nicholas II and the composer Rimskii-Korsakov, reflected with such finesse the psychology of his subjects. Russian creative art, freed at last from all constraint, offered its greatest promise when the communist tyranny interrupted its positive development, as it did in literature and so many other aspects of the country's life.

Friendly relationships between men and women were considered quite normal and did not encounter the obstacles which prevailed in so many countries at that time, and which still endure among the Latin peoples. It was not in any way frowned upon if a woman went out alone with one of her male friends or with one of her husband's friends to the theater. There was nothing compromising in such behavior. A man could invite a lady to dine in his home or at a restaurant without her husband, if he was absent or otherwise occupied, although this was not usually done without inviting one or more other ladies for the sake of appearances. Every well-bred man was considered capable of appreciating such confidence and of being aware of the responsibility thus incurred. These customs made life more free and agreeable and in no way disturbed the stability of families.

The same freedom did not extend to young women. The men were raised to give absolute respect to unmarried girls. An officer who seduced one automatically risked expulsion from his regiment and exclusion from society. A man of the world never showed himself in public with a courtesan, or even with a mistress. Consequently, the most sought-after demimondaines never appeared in public accompanied by men.

Most marriages were based on mutual inclination, not on considerations of wealth, but the social status of the parties strongly entered the picture. Divorce, while extant, was rarely practiced. Women in Russia had exactly the same civil rights as men; daughters had the same inheritance rights as sons. In well educated circles, the girls, like their brothers, generally did not marry until they had completed their secondary education. As regards the higher education of women, Russia even at this period was ahead of the countries of Western Europe: on the eve of the war in 1914, there were 50,000 women in Russian institutions of higher learning.

During the three years I spent in Paris as secretary of the Russian embassy—from 1908 to 1911—I witnessed the beginnings of aviation, and was profoundly interested by this innovation.

The first experimenters with heavier-than-air machines—the American Wilbur Wright and the Brazilian Alberto Santos-Dumont—had already succeeded in getting off the ground and staying aloft for short periods of time.* In 1908 two important events in the history of aviation took place in France: Henri Farman, a Frenchman, made a flight of an hour and a quarter over Issy-les-Moulineaux, near Paris; and Wilbur Wright stayed in the air at Mans for an hour and a half. Both flew biplanes of their own construction at speeds of about 60 kilometers an hour. To these successes were added the historic crossing of the Channel, from Calais to Dover on July 25, 1909, by another Frenchman, Louis Blériot, in his little monoplane. These exploits made a great impression on several of my compatriots who realized immediately how important the new-born field of aviation would be in national defense. The Grand Duke Alexander Mikhailovich, a cousin of the Emperor and a man with an open mind, was won over to the idea of providing the Army and the Navy with the recently invented airplanes. In order to make a reality of the project, he gathered about him a small group of young men, including my excellent friend Vasilii Soldatenkov, a naval officer. As the competent authorities proved unready to act rapidly and to grant sufficient credit, it was decided that a private subscription would be undertaken to secure the funds needed to buy the most appropriate planes, which would then be presented to the armed forces. With imperial consent, a committee was constituted for this purpose under the chairmanship of the Grand Duke. Some members of this committee made the first contributions, while others helped by working to raise funds.

* The first flight of Wilbur Wright took place in the United States in 1903 and lasted 59 seconds. The next year, he stayed aloft for 38 minutes. Santos-Dumont achieved his first flights—also of brief duration—in Paris in 1905 and 1906.

I had many opportunities to see Santos-Dumont. In spite of his unimpressive appearance, this small man attracted the sympathetic attention of the public all over the world for his perseverance, his courage, and his exploits, all of which were enhanced by his natural modesty.

I was at that moment on leave in St. Petersburg. The Grand Duke Alexander and his wife the Grand Duchess Xenia (the Emperor's sister) invited me to luncheon. The Grand Duke asked me to join his committee and to assume the unpaid position of representative in Western Europe, particularly in Paris, which had become the center of the fledgling aircraft industry. I was assigned an engineer, Rebikov, as an aide, as well as a technical officer.

When I returned to Paris, I used what time I had free from the embassy to study the practical aspects of all the aircraft that were flown in these heroic years of aviation. I decided to participate myself in their trial flights, a task for which I was not contested by my assistants.

At that time, all aircraft were open; the first ones did not even have cabins. In winter the cold, which was made worse by wind from the propeller, was painful, in spite of the relatively low speed of the planes, which could not go faster than 50 to 80 kilometers per hour. No plane could carry more than two persons—the pilot and one passenger. The first engines, such as the three-cylinder Anzani, which developed 25 hp., were lubricated with cod-liver oil, and during flight the occupants of the plane had their faces and clothes abundantly sprayed with this nauseating product.*

My first flight was on an Astra biplane, a French model of the Wilbur Wright craft. It had a single engine, designed by Wright, with two propellers, one on each wing, which turned in opposite directions. The takeoff required a launching mechanism; there were skids for the landing. I sat on a small board supported by two thin beams inside the front of the plane. We circled the airport several times, and during the descent

* The engines were still very heavy in relation to their power output; consequently, the weight of the airplane bodies had to be reduced to a minimum. The body was generally made of wooden struts with canvas covering. The engines improved little by little, permitting increased speed and more solid construction. The Gnôme motor, a rotary model invented by the Séguin brothers, made one of the greatest contributions to this progress.

the plane angled in too steeply—out of control—and the
pilot could not right its angle. I saw the ground speeding up
to meet us. Fortunately we were at a low altitude. The engine
was right behind me. Not wishing to be crushed when we hit
the ground, I pulled myself up onto one wing. The light wood,
canvas, and wire structure of the biplane absorbed enough of
the shock in breaking up to allow pilot and passenger to get
away with only a few bruises.

I later visited the Bréguet brothers, Louis and Jacques, at
Douai. These two engineers—good-looking, well-bred, dignified men descended from a family of scholars—made an excellent impression on me. At that time they had only a simple
workshop and a small hangar. They took me on a tour over
Douai and I was able to appreciate the fine performance of
their biplane. After several days of reflection and comparing
the plane with others, I ordered the first three Bréguet planes
that were sent to Russia. Louis Bréguet, with whom I was to
form a lasting friendship, always called me his "first client."

Next I tried the Farman biplanes at Buc, near Paris. In the
design of these clearly good planes the propeller was placed
behind the wings.* My attention also was drawn to the mono-
planes of Louis Blériot, an engineer who had been a manu-
facturer of automobile headlights. I went a number of times
to Etampes, where Blériot had his workshops and his testing
strip, and where he flew me in his planes. We immediately
bought several of them. Unfortunately, one of his best pilots
died in a Blériot airplane shortly thereafter during an air show.
Blériot had neither the scientific background nor the charm
of Louis Bréguet. He was a somewhat severe personality, but
his integrity and his unlimited energy compelled respect.

Then I tried the little Coudron biplane. Its builder flew
me over the Somme estuary, and I felt completely secure dur-

---

* Farman then maintained that it was more important to reduce air
resistance in front than to reduce the weight of the plane, and that it
was necessary to augment the power of the engine without worrying
too much about excess weight. He was right.

ing all its maneuvers. I could not say the same for the aircraft built by a man named Train, who invited me to take a flight with him outside of Paris. His little monoplane had between its wings only one seat, for the pilot. Under the fuselage was a steel bar that extended vertically into the void and ended in a curve to which was attached a bicycle seat. That was the passenger's seat! Train cautioned me to keep a good grip on the bar, which was my only connection to the airplane. I have certainly never enjoyed such complete ground visibility from the air, but on the other hand the body of the plane blocked my view above and isolated me from the pilot. The craft had great difficulty in gaining altitude. As we were flying low over green fields, I spotted a high-tension line in front of us. Train shouted, "Pull up your legs, pull up your legs!" I did so, and we just made it over the cables.

Several days later, poor Train did not have such luck. At an air show being held in Paris—I do not recall whether it was on the Esplanade of the Invalides or at the Champs de Mars —the aircraft piloted by Train, the same one I had been in, came down on M. Berteaux, the minister of war, and killed him.

There were also other aircraft that appeared in France during this period. The Morane monoplane and the Voisin biplane both had many good points, and both enjoyed a certain success. The Latham monoplane was made entirely of wood and had flexible wings, but it turned out to be too unwieldy and impractical. Latham tried to cross the Channel shortly after Blériot, but was forced down in the water.

Of all the aircraft that I saw and tried, the Nieuport biplane pleased me most. This plane, which was built a bit later than the first ones I tried, was clearly representative of progress. I wanted to become thoroughly familiar with it and asked Eduard Nieuport to take me up several times in different weather conditions and at different altitudes. I thus satisfied myself that the plane had excellent stability and fine control in all situations, with the engine running or in a

glide. Nieuport had such confidence in this plane that he ran
it through the most severe tests with me sitting behind him to
see all he did. When he wanted to show me the security of
his plane, he climbed for altitude and then tore out the wires
leading to the engine so that he could not again start it in the
air. Then he banked over a wingtip, put the plane into a spin,
and straightened out at the last moment. Nieuport accomplished this feat several times, with me aboard, over the air-
field at Villacoublay near Paris. Alas, one day this brave man
was doing the same acrobatic feat, pulled out too late, and
crashed to the ground as his wife and little boy looked on
aghast. With his untimely death aviation suffered a great loss.
I regretted his death all the more because he was an extremely
likeable person. Orders for Nieuport planes were the biggest
I made for our committee. It was in a Nieuport that a Russian
officer, Nesterov, did a loop-the-loop for the first time.

The English followed the example of France and also began to build airplanes. I wanted to evaluate the new Bristol
airplanes and went to Salisbury. There I stayed in a typical
old English provincial inn, where I ate nothing but roast beef
and potatoes. I made several flights around the towers of the
beautiful cathedral, followed by maneuvers and altitude tests.
The Bristol planes displayed some decided advtanges, so we
bought several of them.

I was recalled to Russia in 1911 and had to end my mission
for the "Special Committee for the Purchase of Airplanes for
the Armed Forces with Voluntary Contributions." All together, nearly 350 airplanes had been bought or ordered as
a result of my efforts. Most of them, especially the Nieuports,
did useful service as reconnaissance aircraft for the Russian
Army during the First World War.

— 3 —

Fateful Years

The struggle against autocracy was carried on by individuals or small groups until 1905; it was only in that year that the masses were drawn into one vast movement. The broadening of revolutionary activity was caused by an unsuccessful war, economic difficulties, and the intensification of subversive propaganda.

The rapid industrial growth of the last decade of the nineteenth century had slowed down, and by 1903 strikes occurred more frequently. Urged on by students who shared their social-democratic ideas, the workers began demonstrating in the streets and for the first time put forward claims of a political nature. Unrest grew in the universities. Terrorists of the socialist-revolutionary party increased their assassinations of leading members of the administration: in 1904 Minister of the Interior V. K. Plehve, one of those chiefly responsible for the war with Japan, was murdered. The *zemstvos* were voicing demands for liberal reforms, and similar wishes were expressed by lawyers, doctors, writers, and engineers who began to form professional unions.

In the meantime, the Russian outlook in the war with Japan, which had started in February 1904 and was an unpopular cause from the beginning, was steadily worsening. The Japanese seizure of Port Arthur on February 15, 1905, had a depressing impact on the entire country, and each new military reverse diminished the prestige of the government in the

45

opinion of the educated classes and intensified the unrest of the masses.

On January 22, 1905, tragic events took place in St. Petersburg. It was Sunday, a clear, cold day. As soon as I left my residence I noticed many troops stationed in the streets. I saw some officers whom I knew and asked them the reason for these precautions. They told me they were expecting big demonstrations by the workers, who wanted to go to the Palace Place to present their grievances to the Emperor. I learned also that large crowds had formed in the neighborhood of the big Putilov metal works. I decided to go there to see what was happening.

I arrived toward noon at a square surrounding a triumphal arch commemorating the battle of Narva. A huge procession was pouring into the square, led by a priest in vestments carrying a cross in his hand. I later learned that this was Father Georgii Gapon, and that the crowd which followed him numbered about 30,000 persons. At the head of the procession people carried church banners, icons, and a large portrait of the Emperor. The group around the priest was bareheaded, and sang "Lord, Save Your Faithful," one of the most beautiful hymns of the Russian church. Some red flags were visible farther back. Revolutionary songs rang forth from time to time in the rear ranks. Among the workers in the crowd were young persons who must have been students. The square was blocked by two companies of infantry, one detachment of cavalry, and another of Cossacks. Some officers had come forward and were trying to persuade the crowd to disperse. They were met with cries of protest. Then there was a formal dispersal order with an accompanying trumpet call. The crowd did not obey. There was a salvo. At the instant when the soldiers shouldered their guns, the crowd threw itself down. Later those who could, got up and fled. Many dead and injured lay on the ground.

Shaken by the horrible scene I had just witnessed, I sped to the home of Petr N. Durnovo, who was then undersecretary of state for the interior and happened to be the father of one of my good friends from the Alexander Lycée. He had not expected bloodshed, and was surprised by what I told him. Then he scolded me for walking into the middle of the tumult and called me an imprudent young man. I was to earn such a reprimand once again that day: in the afternoon I drew fire at the corner of Nevsky Prospect and Moika.

In the course of the day many more persons were killed and wounded. It was only several days later that I had an explanation of this tragedy. The mobilization of the masses, which was the salient feature of that day which came to be known as "Bloody Sunday," had not been planned or even desired by the revolutionaries. A police functionary named Zubatov had conceived the idea of organizing workers' groups to aid the laborers in their quest for better conditions. In supporting the workers' movement he thought he could keep it under control and prevent it from falling under the influence of the socialist parties. Father Gapon, an ambitious priest and an excellent orator, was placed at the head of the new organization. But instead of following the instructions of the police who had put him in power, Gapon decided to lead his followers to the Imperial Palace in a peaceful demonstration to present to the Tsar certain demands which were clearly political in character as well as economic. The petition stating these demands was signed by 135,000 persons.

According to the information I was able to gather, no one in government circles had wanted the army to shoot upon a crowd that had committed no act of violence; the tragedy simply resulted from the fact that the soldiers failed to maintain their composure. The events of January 22 were even more deplorable because they had their origin not in a revolutionary action but in an unwonted initiative of the police. This cruel and useless massacre had enormous repercussions throughout the country. The shock and resentment it provoked among the masses dealt a heavy blow to their faith in the Tsar, the "little father" of the people.

The immediate consequence of "Bloody Sunday" was an

intensification of revolutionary activities and an increase of disturbances. Strikes grew in number and scope. Agrarian unrest spread through the entire country. The Grand Duke Sergei Alexandrovich was assassinated in Moscow. Intellectuals who had formed diverse professional unions now joined in a federation called the "Union of Unions" with Professor Pavel N. Miliukov as their president. The congress of *zemstvos,* through its representative Prince Sergei Trubetskoi, implored the Tsar to call for a national representation elected by all his subjects. Finally, disregarding the restrictive laws that held it in check, the press joined the opposition movement.

With the nationwide consternation and resentment against the government engendered by the destruction of the Russian fleet by the Japanese at Tsushima (May 27–28, 1905), all those who opposed the regime, from extremists to moderates, became united. In the Black Sea, the crew of the cruiser *Potemkin* mutinied (I saw the vessel bombarding Odessa when I stayed there for a short time in July 1905).

Hoping to subdue the revolutionary agitation—and at the urging of his minister of finance, Vladimir N. Kokovtsov, Nicholas II commissioned Minister of the Interior Alexander G. Bulygin to submit a draft of a law creating a Duma, or Assembly, to be elected on the basis of income qualification and limited in its authority to a consultative role. The announcement of this reform satisfied no one.

In the meantime Witte, the most capable man in the administration, had been sent to the United States to negotiate with the Japanese. He succeeded in concluding an honorable peace on September 5, 1905, and for this achievement was rewarded with the title of Count.

The internal situation deteriorated rapidly. The revolutionaries were preparing a concerted general movement, and a railroad strike proclaimed on October 20 spread over the whole country until by October 23 it had become a general strike that paralyzed the entire life of the Empire. The leadership of the extreme left wing of the movement was in the hands of a council of delegates of workers and socialist parties which had convened in St. Petersburg and assumed the fateful name of Soviet.* The administration was powerless and bewildered.

To save the situation Nicholas II called in Witte as soon as he returned from his triumph in America. Witte drafted a manifesto declaring that Russia would be transformed into a constitutional monarchy. The Grand Duke Nicholas warned that he would commit suicide if the Tsar ordered him to crush the popular uprising instead of following Witte's wise advice.

The Emperor resigned himself to the "dreadful decision," and the manifesto was published October 30. In it the Tsar promised to guarantee the inviolability of person as well as freedom of conscience, of speech, and of reunion and association. He further vowed to establish the inviolable principle that no law would be valid without the approbation of a Duma constituted by the representatives of the nation, and that this Duma would assure the legality of actions of the administration. Finally, the document declared that the right to vote would be extended to all classes in the nation. This historic decision produced immense joy in liberal circles and filled my heart with hope.

By dividing the opposition, the promise of a constitution restored the government's power to act. The liberal bourgeoisie, satisfied that the government had taken the road to concessions, split with the socialist activists, who in turn increased their efforts in the hope of achieving a social upheaval. The government, now with Witte at its head, regained public confidence and vigorously suppressed the revolutionary activity of the socialists. This repression was carried out with unfaltering energy by Durnovo, who now was the minister of the interior. Military contingents put an end to numerous and bloody agrarian uprisings. Police arrested the leaders of the Peasant Union when they convened in Moscow and demanded the expropriation of private estates. Then the St. Petersburg Soviet was dispersed and its executive committee arrested.

* Soviet means "Council" in Russian.

When a violent insurrection erupted in Moscow it was crushed
by loyal troops after a few days of street fighting. Several
mutinies in the Army and Navy were liquidated with similar
dispatch.

By the end of February 1906 the revolutionary thrust was
broken up throughout the country. But it was to have a long-
lasting effect: it had uprooted secular prejudices and awakened
millions of peasants and workers to the possibilities inherent
in political struggle.

Soon thereafter a wave of reaction swept the country. A
group belonging to the extreme right, organized under the
name League of the Russian People and supported by the
police, recruited gangs of ruffians, the so-called "black hundreds," who indulged in extremely violent outbursts against
what they termed the "enemies of the people"—socialists, intellectuals, Jews—all the while claiming to be defenders of
autocracy. No worse service could have been rendered the
monarchy. We were repulsed by such villainy and desired
even more strongly to see the new regime established on solid
foundations.

The principles proclaimed in the manifesto of October 30
were not sufficient in themselves to effect the promised reforms: they had to be translated into definite measures. Witte
accomplished this by formulating the laws to establish a new
structure for the Empire, the "Fundamental Laws" of 1906.
A profoundly realistic man, he understood that it would be impossible to maintain the autocratic regime as it existed, but
conservative prudence induced him to preserve the imperial
prerogatives at least for the time being. The result was a
hybrid constitution that confined the national representation
within narrow limits and permitted the survival of a vast
zone of influence belonging exclusively to the crown.

The word "constitution" did not even appear in the text
of this document. On the insistence of Nicholas II the term
"autocrat" remained in the Tsar's title. Witte attempted to

justify this incongruity with the excuse that in old Russia the word was used to attest to the independence of the ruler when he dealt with foreign powers.

The new order offered neither direct and universal suffrage nor the kind of parliamentarism that would imply an executive power dependent on the will of a majority of a legislative chamber. The ministers were always appointed by the sovereign and were responsible to him alone. The following years were to demonstrate that this right of choosing ministers gave the crown a decisive advantage. The Army, the Navy, and the diplomatic corps were, as before, accountable only to the Emperor. And in accordance with Article 87 of the Fundamental Laws the crown also reserved the right to legislate alone, if necessary, during intervals between the sessions of the Duma, under condition that laws thus promulgated be submitted to the Chamber when it reconvened.

Notwithstanding all these restrictions imposed on the national representation, however, the Duma obtained wide powers with respect to legislative and budgetary matters. Experience proved that in course of its discussions of the budget the Duma could discuss any question. Moreover it could exercise its right of summons and demand explanations from the ministers. The former Council of State was transformed into an Upper Chamber with half of its members still appointed by the Tsar and the other half elected by the *zemstvos,* the nobility, the clergy, the universities, commerce, and industry.

As to elections to the Duma, the law regulating them guaranteed their freedom and created a large electorate representing all the classes of the population. Owing to a system of second- and third-degree suffrage, different groups of voters had different and unequal numbers of votes; * still, the peasants obtained an important number of delegates in the elec-

* The franchise was given only to those who could prove they possessed certain minimal financial assets, but the required sum was so small that almost the entire population was able to vote.

toral assemblies inasmuch as the "high spheres" still saw them as children devoted and obedient to their "little father," the Tsar.

Of course the liberal circles—not to mention the socialists —had hoped for a more democratic constitution. Yet the regime established in 1906 represented a tremendous advancement from the past and could have been a first stage, and a perfectly viable one, along the road of constitutional evolution.

Nicholas II had never liked Witte. He had always sensed the superiority of this ambitious and authoritarian man and was shocked by the rudeness of his manners. But now he could not forgive Witte for having urged him to endorse the surrender of the principle of autocracy. Having lost confidence in his prime minister, the Emperor henceforth would make no further decision without consulting the Palace commandant, General Dmitrii Trepov, a man whose often ambivalent political ideas were definite on at least one point: his loyalty to the monarchy. As soon as the revolutionary movement appeared to be under control, Nicholas II dismissed Witte.* This he did only five days before the first session of the Duma.

The opening session of the First Duma took place on May 10, 1906, a beautiful spring day. Before the session the deputies were received by the Emperor at the Winter Palace. Since I was attached to the Court, I assisted at that ceremony, and have retained a vivid memory of it. The deputies were a heterogeneous group. The frock coats of intellectuals could be seen side by side with peasant dress, the picturesque costumes of various non-Russian nationalities, the black cassocks of

* Witte had made a thorough study of the agrarian problem. After the promulgation of the manifesto of October 30, he proceeded, with the assistance of the minister of agriculture, Nikolai N. Kutler, to develop a project of agrarian reform through compulsory redemption of a part of the private estates and distribution of the redeemed lands to the peasants. The strong objections of the "Union of the Nobility" to Witte's initiative contributed to his downfall, and after that he never again played an important role in Russian politics.

priests. This was the new Russia, whose simple but dignified appearance contrasted strikingly with the courtiers of the old regime dressed in sparkling uniforms and bedizened with decorations. The Emperor welcomed the deputies and finished his speech with a declaration that he would guarantee the unshakeable continuity of the newly created institutions. The audience was filled with optimism. This state of mind was of short duration.

The new premier, President of the Council Ivan L. Goremykin, was a staunch bureaucrat of no real worth. He was an old fox, at home amid all the wheels of the administrative machinery of the vast Empire and a master in the art of advancing through them. He was not without a certain kind of intelligence, but being quite bereft of vision he was naturally opposed to any change lest it cause the collapse of the whole system of his ideas. He solved all problems by total and passive obedience to the Tsar's orders. This old man with white sideburns showed no desire to collaborate with the Duma. When he was present at the meetings of the Chamber, he tended to fall asleep in his ministerial seat. When he was obliged to ascend the rostrum he read his speeches in a voice so weak as to be scarcely audible and grew confused at the most important passages. It seems incredible that ten years later, during the First World War, this evil and by then completely wrecked old man would be called again to head the government, and that at a time of even greater crisis.

The First Duma was distinctly oriented to the left. Its most powerful party was the party of Constitutional Democrats, or "Cadets." It contained the most cultured minds and was born in 1905 from the "Union for Liberation" which united liberals from the *zemstvos* and the professions. They were all men opposed to autocracy as well as to social revolution. The program of the Cadets had as its goals constitutional monarchy, civil rights, religious and racial equality, protection of industrial workers, and expropriation of private estates for the benefit of the peasants but with fair compensation to the owners.

The most remarkable personality in the Cadets' party was Professor Pavel N. Miliukov. Another member of that party, Muromtsev, my former professor of civil law at the Alexander Lycée, was elected president of the Duma.

The second and third power positions were held by groups of the independents and representatives of the Workers' Party.

The revolutionary parties had a weak representation. The Social Democrats as well as the Socialist Revolutionaries had boycotted the elections to protest the insufficiently democratic character of the franchise. But they had not been able to prevent the working classes from voting, which proves how little influence they had over them at that time. The peasants and workers gave some of their votes to the Cadets, but most of them backed independents and Workers' Party candidates. Thus the peasants managed to occupy almost half of the seats in the Chamber.

Finally, the Duma also contained a group of moderate conservatives who belonged to the "Party of October 30," or the Octobrists.* Their leader was Dmitrii N. Shipov, who was later succeeded by Alexander Guchkov. Though the Octobrists formed the extreme right of the Chamber, they represented by virtue of their attachment to the new constitution and their desire to strengthen it a tendency that was more to the left than the administration, which seemed already to regret its concessions.

The Duma united at once in an attitude of opposition to the government. With the Cadets leading the dance, the Chamber launched forth with a violent indictment of the regime and demanded a revision of the new Fundamental Laws, asserting that they violated the freedoms promised by the October 30 manifesto.

The predominance of the peasant element in the Duma

* The name assumed by this party was meant to indicate that they would be satisfied with the sincere application and logical development of the promises contained in the manifesto of October 30, 1905 (see p. 49).

compelled concentrated attention on the agrarian question. It was on this point that the government made its greatest mistake. Speaking through Goremykin, it made it clear that it would absolutely oppose any proposal for expropriation of privately owned land for the benefit of the peasants. Then, on July 22, 1906, deeming this Chamber too radical for effective collaboration, the government dissolved it. It had lasted less than two and a half months.

The First Duma had deep roots in the popular masses and correctly expressed their feelings. The government's refusal to cooperate with it had tremendous repercussions. Now the centuries-old faith of the peasants in the Tsar and autocrat, already shaken by "Bloody Sunday," was definitely destroyed. In a letter addressed to the Emperor, Prince Evgenii Trubetskoi, the brother of my good friend and colleague Prince Grigorii Trubetskoi, attempted to point out to the Sovereign the importance of that mistake. He wrote:

It is with unspeakable anguish that I observe the transformation that grows more profound every hour, every day in the minds and feelings of the people. If you could only hear, Sire, what the peasants sing while they work in the fields. Only two or three months ago they would have torn to pieces anyone who dared to sing such songs. . . . As recently as the last elections, the popular sentiment was altogether different. Then the people were going to send their elected representatives to confide their needs to their Tsar. . . . They still felt close to him. They had faith in him despite the propaganda of the revolutionaries who would go to any lengths to sever the ties between the sovereign and his subjects. And yet what that propaganda failed to achieve was realized—by the worst enemies of Your Majesty, by your own advisers. . . . There is an irresistible force in the desire of the peasants to possess more land. . . . Refusal to grant them this was, in their opinion, the only cause of the dissolution of the Duma. Even worse, your advisers have placed the responsibility for rejection of the peasants' aspirations on your shoulders. Thus they have succeeded in transforming the agrarian problem into a dynastic one. . . . I see with terror the abyss that opens before you.

The author of this letter, one of the most eminent scholars at the University of Moscow and a sincere supporter of the monarchy, did not make his message public. I was one of the few persons who knew about it at that time.

By an agreement to distribute the lands of the great landowners to the peasants in exchange for an indemnity, Nicholas II could not only have consolidated his throne; he could even have refused any further political concessions and perhaps retained autocratic power for a few decades. Suggestions in that direction were made to him, but he did not heed them. I learned that in May 1905 General Dmitrii Trepov submitted to the Emperor the letter of a certain I. J. Hofstaetter. This letter was truly prophetic. I quote the main passages:

> One can predict with certainty that either the Russian monarchy will become deeply and consciously democratic or in ten years there will be no trace of the monarchy in Russia. It will have completely lost its historic prestige in the eyes of the hundred million peasants whose blind faith still permits it to stand despite the fierce hostility of the educated classes, or it will have restored its faltering prestige by a new act of pure devotion to the people's cause, an act comparable in the popular memory to the unforgettable action of 1861 (i.e., the emancipation of the serfs). Only a vast agrarian reform accomplished in the interests of the whole of the Russian people could qualify as such an act. At the point where we stand today, only measures of that kind can save the dynasty from disaster and the educated class from total destruction.

If Nicholas II never considered the possibility of taking the road that would certainly have saved him, it was because, always loyal to the traditions of his education, he did not want to turn his back on the nobility which he had been taught to regard as the firm support of the monarchy. He also closed his eyes to the fact that the strength of the nobility was greatly reduced and the support they could offer to the crown was nothing but illusion. Therefore it is not surprising that he listened with favor when the "Union of the Nobility" protested against all infringement of the landed patrimony still remaining in the hands of the gentry. This Union, formed in 1905 by reactionary members of the nobility, did not realize that from the point of view of their own class interests an expropriation with indemnity was much preferable to complete spoliation, as Prince Trubetskoi pointed out in his above-quoted letter.

The task of dissolving the First Duma passed to Petr A. Stolypin,* who was considered a man of energy and decision and thus was called to the post of prime minister to replace the inept Goremykin. The opposition—Cadets, members of the Workers' Party, and socialists—met at Viborg, in Finland, under the chairmanship of Muromtsev and drafted an impassioned appeal to the nation to protest the dissolution of the Duma. Stolypin replied to that challenge by declaring those who had signed the appeal ineligible for candidacy in the elections for the new Duma. For want of sufficient organization of public opinion, the Viborg appeal did not produce the expected reaction in the country, although there were some agrarian disturbances and mutinies in the armed forces.

Stolypin next took vigorous measures to crush what remained of the revolutionary movement. Sixteen hundred state officials were killed by terrorists in 1906, twenty-five hundred in 1907, and those who were guilty of these crimes could not be executed because the Russian criminal law did not provide for capital punishment. Stolypin circumvented this obstacle by establishing courts-martial. They remained active for only a matter of months, but in that time the revolutionary spirit,

* Petr A. Stolypin was a lawyer and statesman who had been in high administrative posts before he was named minister of the interior in May 1906. In July 1906 he became premier of Russia. He was assassinated in 1911. (Editor's note.)

already weakened by the repression of the disturbances of 1905–1906, was broken. The country was weary of disorder, the political parties were unable to create a unified movement, and the decimated revolutionaries crawled underground to await more favorable circumstances.

Stolypin did not possess Witte's intelligence, but during the reign of Nicholas II he was second only to Witte as a statesman. He combined great courage and absolute integrity with a clear and practical intelligence and an unselfish dedication to his task. Being resolute, he also did not shirk certain brutal measures. My memory has preserved a picture of the man when with his natural and direct eloquence, and in a powerful voice, he delivered a speech in the Duma. This country gentleman was then at the peak of his powers and made a commanding appearance with his high forehead and black beard. His intention was to adhere firmly to the principles of monarchy and public order, but—more daring than his predecessors—he had resolved to make a bold attack on the agrarian problem, having correctly divined its importance. Deeply attached to Russian religious and national traditions, Stolypin was tolerant of nationalistic tendencies inside the Empire; on the other hand he was firmly opposed to allowing Russia to entertain national ambitions that could endanger international peace. He supported the newly established constitutional regime, but he did not favor any extension of the Duma's authority. He wanted to collaborate with the Duma, but under the condition that it would not attempt to foment revolution.

Stolypin started out by offering some of the ministerial portfolios in his cabinet to moderate liberals, but he found the conditions they set for acceptance too harsh. In this the liberals committed the same mistake as they had in 1905 when they refused to join Witte's cabinet. Had they been more realistic and less dogmatic, they might have found that collaboration with the bureaucratic machine could be fruitful, and they would have remained free to abandon it if it proved impossible.

The Second Duma convened in March 1907. Notwithstanding the pressures exerted on the electorate, it was more radical than the First because the socialists had abandoned their tactic of boycotting the elections. Following the advice of the Cadets, the new deputies took certain cautionary measures to avoid exposing the Duma to another dissolution, but their efforts were unavailing. The introduction from the rostrum of projects tending toward expropriation of large estates again gave rise to alarm in the Union of the Nobility, who in turn persuaded Stolypin to find a pretext for dismissing the Assembly and electing a less radical Chamber. The desired opportunity soon arose.

Several socialist deputies were implicated in revolutionary activities, and when the Duma refused to suspend their parliamentary immunity it was dissolved on June 16, 1907, after only three months' existence. On the same day, through a misapplication of Article 87 of the Fundamental Laws, the electoral law was changed by an imperial edict that gave the landed gentry and other conservative elements a prevailing influence. To serve that end, the new electoral laws allowed the minister of the interior to manipulate the limits of electoral districts and the distribution of electors in various groups in such a way as to give the advantage to the pro-regime minority and at the same time weaken the representation of the rural and city masses. The electoral reform was also detrimental to the country's non-Russians, particularly the Poles.

The Third Duma (1907–1912), like the Fourth which followed it (1912–1917), was elected according to the same limited-franchise principles and was a poor reflection of the state of mind of the country. The peasants deeply resented such unfair treatment and dubbed the new Chamber the "Duma of great landowners." In that Assembly the nationalists, who were the natural support of the government, obtained one-third of the seats; the Octobrists claimed another third. The last third consisted of leftists and a small number of representatives of national minorities—mostly Poles—who often voted with the opposition. The left was represented mainly by the K.D. Party and by small groups of Workers' Party delegates and Social Democrats.

As this Chamber was elected mainly by the educated classes, it included many remarkable men, such as the Octobrist leader Alexander Guchkov; the K.D. Party's great historian Miliukov, its brilliant orator Vasilii Maklakov, and its public finance specialist Andrei I. Shingarev; the nationalist Vasilii V. Shulgin; the socialist Nikolai S. Chkheidze. All these men were to play important roles later.

A collaboration was established between Stolypin and the Octobrists, and the majority of the Assembly agreed to the nationalist policy of Stolypin. Alleging superior interests of the Empire, the Duma passed a law which imposed important limitations on the autonomy of Finland.* The territory of Kholm, which was inhabited by a mostly non-Polish population, was detached from the Polish provinces. New restrictions were applied to the Jews.

The Third Duma also ratified agrarian legislation which Stolypin had introduced by decree, without awaiting the approbation of the Chambers, always craftily using Article 87 of the Fundamental Laws.

Stolypin saw the solution of the agrarian problem not in a repartition among the peasants of great estates still in the hands of the nobility, but rather in an improvement of the mode of tenure of lands already assigned to the peasantry. In his opinion the communal ownership of land fostered in the peasant a desire to remain on the same level with all other peasants and prevented the most active and able ones from improving their condition and thus contributing to the growth of the general welfare and the development of production. Proceeding from this viewpoint, he would "bet on the strong ones," according to an expression he used at that time.

This was exactly opposite to the program of the socialists

---

* The Finns had never created any serious difficulties for Russia; the Cadets defended them with energy from the Duma rostrum.

and revolutionaries, who wanted to preserve the commune, which they saw as a preliminary stage on the road to modern socialism. The new laws allowed any peasant to have his land allotment detached from the collective and transformed into personal and hereditary property. If, as unfortunately was often the case, his allotment consisted of widely separated lots, he could request that it be in one contiguous piece. Moreover, the village assemblies were authorized to distribute the entire local collectively owned land in as many individual properties as there were family heads; a majority of votes of commune members was sufficient to adopt a decision to this end. This reform achieved amazingly successful results, which proved that it satisfied a natural tendency. In the ten-year period from 1906 to 1916 three million peasant homesteaders (i.e., 20 percent of the total number) repudiated the communal system and obtained individual lots.

The result of Stolypin's agrarian laws was the growth of a thin layer of enterprising and well-to-do peasants.* On the other hand, those who remained in the commune found themselves in a worse situation than before. These two groups of peasants were fated to confront each other face to face in the social conflicts that lay ahead.

This notwithstanding, if Stolypin's reform had not been checked by the war, it might have succeeded in stabilizing social conditions in Russia by stimulating prosperity and a respect for private property through the establishment of a new and sizable class of small landowners. This is of course merely a conjecture, and it merits consideration only if one assumes that the government would have adopted a more enlightened internal policy in other fields.

Other measures contributed further to the improvement of the peasants' condition. They had already been released from obligation for the balance of their redemption payments on the lands distributed to them in 1861. Now all the restrictions

* Even before Stolypin's reforms 2,800,000 peasant families had owned their land in personal property.

that had been imposed on their freedom by the rural commune were lifted. The special regime to which they were still
subject was therefore disappearing. Moreover, Stolypin's
agrarian measures greatly contributed to the development of
the cooperative movement. As peasants became masters of
their fields in greater numbers, they attempted to get together
with other farmers of similar motivation to acquire needed
farm implements and sell their products. Indeed, the rise of
the cooperative movement was spectacular if one considers
the brief time span it was granted by history. The success of
the cooperatives was assured because they were patterned
after the English model and thus exercised the principle of
complete freedom of association.

In spite of its conservative spirit, the Third Duma also laid
particular stress on the development of mass education.
Thanks to legislative measures it voted, a progressive compulsory education plan was instigated that was to have reached
all children in the nation by 1922.

The Stolypin cabinet had some men of moral and intellectual value. Alexander V. Krivoshein, the minister of agriculture, would carry on the agrarian reform. At foreign affairs Stolypin's brother-in-law, Sergei Sazonov, a model of integrity, inspired the confidence of friendly nations. Vladimir
N. Kokovtsov, the minister of finance who had been one of
Witte's assistants, managed the finances of the Empire with
great wisdom and thus helped to bring to Russia during the
seven years before the war the greatest prosperity she had
ever known. These ministers kept up good relations with the
Duma, which for its part was gaining greater familiarity with
the practice of statesmanship and beginning to provide a good
training ground for competence in its commissions.

By virtue of the Octobrist Party's predominant influence in
the Third Duma, Alexander Guchkov was bound to play an
important role: he was elected president of the Duma. This
daring fighter was born in 1860, grandson of a serf and the
son of a Moscow merchant. He never ceased to be inspired

by ardent patriotism. He had a wonderful talent for organizing and liked to stride ahead and attack current problems head on. His courage was accompanied by steady self-control. His energetic temperament sometimes pushed him into adventure, and he was attracted by danger. He paid visits to Macedonia and Armenia while they were having disturbances, to China during the Boxer Rebellion.

Having been reared in the belief that England was forever placing obstacles in Russia's way, Guchkov volunteered for service in the army of the Boers during their war against the British. When the English made him a prisoner of war he was so impressed by their fair attitude that he came to admire them and formed a friendship with Winston Churchill who was then in South Africa as war correspondent. Thereafter he retained a great respect for the morality that governed English public life.

During the revolutionary crisis of 1905 he was received by the Tsar and the Tsarina and tried to convince them of the necessity for cooperation with the moderate liberals grouped in the *zemstvos*. His suggestions were limited at that time to the recommendation that a consultative assembly, patterned after the assemblies which convened in Moscow in the sixteenth and seventeenth centuries, be established as a link between the sovereign and the people. Guchkov's first thought then—as it continued to be later—was to preserve the monarchic principle by adapting it to new and changing conditions. It was these ideas with their stamp of enlightened conservatism that guided the formation of the Octobrist Party.

Ever since the time he had been sent by the Red Cross to the battlefields of Manchuria, Guchkov had been deeply interested in the armed forces. Russia's defeat in the war with Japan had made evident the necessity of reorganizing the Army and the Navy. The Third Duma willingly took up this subject during its discussion of the budget. Guchkov, who was president of the Committee for National Defense, took the lead in that debate but did not proceed with sufficient caution.

Several members of the imperial family were inspectors general in various branches of the military establishment. Guchkov argued that in the interest of effective administration such functions should not be entrusted to persons who could not be held responsible. He concluded by asking the grand dukes to resign their positions. The government agreed to confront the problem by limiting the authority of the grand dukes, especially in the matter of contracts for army supplies, but it was not willing to deprive them entirely of their posts.

Guchkov's intervention seemed to the Emperor to be an attack against his prerogatives, for according to the Fundamental Laws of 1906 Army and Navy were amenable only to the sovereign. Guchkov had already irritated Empress Alexandra on an earlier occasion when he insisted that the term "autocrat" should not be used in an address from the Duma to the Tsar.

The Third Duma, which had been so docile at first, finally rebelled against the government. The Octobrists, tired of being used at a tool by Stolypin, drew closer to the Cadets. When Stolypin met opposition from both parties over his proposed law to introduce *zemstvos* in the Western provinces * he lost patience and insisted that the Emperor promulgate this law by an arbitrary misuse of Article 87 of the Fundamental Laws. Guchkov declared that this was an insult to the legislative chambers and renounced the presidency of the Duma. Stolypin also drew the displeasure of the Tsar for having publicly involved him in the matter.

On September 11, 1911, Stolypin was fatally wounded by a revolutionary named Bagrov, and there were rumors that the police had allowed it to happen.

Kokovtsov was appointed president of the Council of Ministers. Since 1906 he had served with great competence as

* The center and the left of the Duma were in favor of granting local self-government to these provinces, but they opposed the government's projects because they considered them unfavorable to the Polish and Jewish minorities.

minister of finance and had shown himself to be a jealous guardian of public funds. He was an intelligent man, scrupulously honest, slightly pedantic, conservative without excess, deeply patriotic and devoted to the service of the state. If he had had some altercations with the Duma, he had always been ready on the whole to cooperate with it.

Unfortunately, Kokovtsov was not a man of strong will, and he was unable to voice opposition when the Emperor appointed to his cabinet certain ministers who were to make his task very difficult indeed. Such was the case of the minister of justice, Ivan G. Shcheglovitov, and later of the minister of the interior, Nikolai A. Maklakov,* both extreme reactionaries.

The Third Duma ended on an anxious note. For several years there had been rumors that an obscure Siberian peasant named Rasputin, a *starets* ** pretending to serve God and spread the good word, had managed to insinuate himself into the intimacy of the imperial couple by taking advantage of the Empress's mystical predilections.

Then it was said that this person was merely a vulgar and uneducated plotter, and that he had gained such a hold over the Tsarina, and through her the Tsar, that his influence was affecting the conduct of the affairs of state and working in a clearly reactionary direction. These reports described Rasputin as a depraved impostor who concealed a life of debauchery and drunkenness behind a facade of piety and virtue. If these rumors had begun to be believed in well-informed St. Petersburg circles, they had still barely penetrated the provinces.

In March 1912 Guchkov and the extreme right-wing rep-

---

* Not to be confused with his brother Vasilii Maklakov, the great liberal orator of the Duma.
** This word was used in Russia to designate an unsophisticated man of ripe age and pious character who practiced his religious convictions by making pilgrimages, by becoming an anchorite, or simply by reciting passages from the Scriptures among the people. This kind of man could be seen frequently in the villages, particularly near churches and monasteries.

resentative Vladimir M. Purishkevich mounted the Duma rostrum to proclaim the true character of this ignoble personality and warn of the danger in his secret dealings in the shadow of the throne. It may seem astonishing that such statements should have been made publicly by two men deeply attached to the monarchy, yet it was precisely their devotion to that principle that moved them to do it. They hoped that their speeches would open the eyes of the imperial couple. Unfortunately, such was the blindness of the Tsar and particularly of the Tsarina that all they saw was hostile intention. Guchkov thereupon became their *bête noire,* although both speakers had tried as far as possible to avoid any criticism directed personally against the sovereigns.

In order to limit the repercussions of these untoward speeches, the administration, aided by the president of the Duma, prevented their publication. But typewritten copies proliferated and the public was informed.

The rumors and revelations concerning Rasputin would certainly have been less damaging to the prestige of the crown if the public had been informed of the tragedy that surrounded the life of the imperial couple. That became known in all its sadness only after the revolution. Empress Alexandra probably would have been judged with more understanding had it been known that in her desperate anxiety over the illness of her young son Alexei, the heir to the throne, she had placed all her hope in some miraculous intercession, and that she had believed her prayers answered when Rasputin, by means which remain mysterious, had twice helped her child through crises that seemed fatal.

The Court concealed the fact that the heir apparent was a victim of hemophilia, against which all medicine was helpless at that time. Unaware of the truth, people who heard about Rasputin indulged in the most absurd conjectures to explain his role behind the scenes at Court.

The Fourth Duma convened in 1912. It was adjourned because of the war and lasted until the revolution of 1917. In the elections the government did not succeed in obtaining a nationalist and reactionary majority capable of supporting it and the opposition grew in number and authority. The Cadets and the extreme left gained some seats; the Octobrists lost some but still remained in command of the situation in the chamber. Mikhail Rodzianko of the Octobrist Party was elected president of the new Duma. A country squire of large and powerful stature, he was distinguished by his fervent patriotism, his sincerity, his absolute integrity, and above all by his great courage. He was also a fine speaker.

A new deputy made his appearance in one of the groups of the extreme left, the "Workers" group. This was Alexander Kerenskii, a young lawyer who had attracted attention by his eloquent defense of persons accused in political trials.

It was not long before friction developed between the government and the Duma. Notwithstanding all his great qualities, Kokovtsov lacked subtlety and consideration for the opinions of others and this did not help his relations with the Duma. As he was generally respected, however, the Chamber's displeasure was not directed so much against him as against his reactionary colleagues and especially against the minister of justice, Shcheglovitov, who combined backward ideas with intelligence and ability in legal matters.

Seconded by the retrograde Moscow journalist, Prince Vladimir P. Meshcherskii, Shcheglovitov started a court intrigue against Kokovtsov. The latter begged the Emperor to give him colleagues who could help him maintain unity in the cabinet. Rather than accede to this wish, the Emperor with his usual amiability dismissed him in February 1914. He was replaced by the servile courtier Goremykin.

My chief, Sergei D. Sazonov, was greatly disappointed at this change. He had great respect for Kokovtsov and a profound antipathy for Goremykin. This seventy-four-year-old man who had already been prime minister after Witte's disgrace was known for his incompetence, his cynicism, and his opposition to any change. According to publications that appeared after the revolution, Kokovtsov's aversion to Rasputin had incurred the enmity of the Empress, and Goremykin's return to the position of prime minister resulted from his own good relations with the evil *starets,* who allegedly interceded in his behalf with the Empress.*

At that time, even if it had been told to me on the highest authority I certainly would not have believed that Rasputin's influence was powerful enough to topple a president of the Council of Ministers and appoint another in his place. What happened behind the scenes in the Palace was a closely guarded secret, and any rumors on that subject that reached us at the Ministry of Foreign Affairs were not to be trusted.** I had to be placed in the immediate circle of the Emperor two years later to realize, little by little, how seriously the exercise of imperial power had been impaired by the intervention of Empress Alexandra, who was herself subject to mysterious influences. It was much later still—after the revolution and after the war—that I learned the whole sad truth, when the letters of Empress Alexandra to Emperor Nicholas were published.

Thus when war broke out in 1914, the Russian government was presided over by Goremykin. His cabinet was composed of men whose worth and political leanings were quite varied.

Vladimir A. Sukhomlinov, the minister of war, had distinguished himself in 1877–1878 as a command officer in the Russo-Turkish war, but inasmuch as he had not revised his ideas to keep up with the modern organization of the Army, his most qualified subordinates judged him unsuited for such a

* If a suggestion made to the Emperor by Minister of Agriculture Krivoshein was the apparent cause of Goremykin's appointment, we must see the true reason for Kokovtsov's removal in the reliance of the Empress on Rasputin's recommendations. Sazonov confirms that in his reminiscences. As for Krivoshein, he soon realized how harmful Goremykin was and turned against him.

** Although Sazonov was always extremely frank with me, he refrained to the end of the monarchy from talking with me about Rasputin despite the fact that the latter never ceased to undermine him. Sazonov's loyalty to his sovereign imposed upon him an absolute silence on this painful subject.

responsible position. Moreover, he was somewhat frivolous and superficial. He had the gift of telling anecdotes and making jokes, and thus had succeeded in entertaining the Emperor, but the Duma did not appreciate him at all. When the vicissitudes of war made clear his incompetence, he was promptly relieved of his functions.

The minister of the interior, Nikolai Maklakov, was a reactionary who accepted the existence of the Duma as a necessary evil and bickered with the *zemstvos*. He had a rather bizarre mentality, which I once had occasion to observe at first hand. When the government of the Kaiser declared war on Russia in August 1914, hostile demonstrations occurred spontaneously in front of the German embassy. The rabble took advantage of these events to break into the embassy building and sack it from top to bottom. Learning that disorders had broken out near the German embassy, Sazonov sent me to see what was happening. I found the pillage and destruction under way, and discovered that the police and the troops who had been requisitioned were not intervening. I found the prefect of police of St. Petersburg, and asked him indignantly to put a stop to this scene of vandalism. He told me that the minister of the interior had just arrived and asked me to talk to him.

I protested to Nikolai Maklakov in the most emphatic terms about the passivity of the police and explained to him that the German embassy was under the protection of the diplomatic representative of the United States. We were obliged to respect the embassy. Moreover, the complicity of Russian officials in acts of pillage would not help our prestige in the eyes of our allies. Maklakov responded that it was necessary to give free rein to the natural furor of the crowd, and that he would limit his role to seeing that the disorders did not spread. When I reported his comments to my superior the latter was not surprised, since he had a low opinion of his colleague at the interior post.

Maklakov, as well as the minister of religion, Vladimir K.

Sabler, another reactionary type—they were both protégés of
Rasputin—became the black sheep of the Duma. The failure
of the reactionary ministers to seek accommodation with the
Duma was even less excusable in view of the fact that the
electoral reform of 1907 had given them the most favorable
majority they could have hoped to find, composed as it was of
cultivated elements of moderate political leanings.

Goremykin and the reactionary members of his cabinet of
course got on badly with those ministers who showed more
wisdom and sought an understanding with the Duma. I have
already had occasion to speak of the pure patriotism and enlightened conservatism of Sazonov. He believed that human
societies, like all living organisms, had to evolve. For him,
this implied a duty to preserve all that was still healthy and
viable and a need to modify, or even to discard, that which
was no longer useful to the social organism. This simple phi-
losophy based on common sense separated Sazonov from
Goremykin and his acolytes and drew him closer to the moderate liberal-Octobrists and the Cadets. I often accompanied
him to sessions of the Duma and saw that he had many sym-
pathizers there. Unfortunately his role as minister of foreign
affairs prevented him from exercising effective influence in
internal policy, and it was only in particularly grave circumstances that he had the opportunity to fight for his ideas.

The minister of agriculture, Krivoshein, was basically an
opportunist, but because he was very intelligent he realized
the dangers that lay in following the road to reaction; he
therefore moved away from Goremykin and associated with
those ministers who hoped to see the government get closer
to the country's liberal elements.

The minister of the Navy, Admiral Ivan K. Grigorovich,
was an excellent man. He contributed greatly to the restoration of the Russian Navy, granted advancement to the most
capable officers, and surrounded himself with honest and competent men. His activity in the Council of Ministers was necessarily limited by the apolitical character of his portfolio, but

his ideas were opposed to reaction. Thus even the Council of Ministers did not escape the conflicts that rent the Russian political scene.

Great changes had taken place in Russia during the ten years between the disorders of 1905 and the war of 1914. Since its emergence the Duma had incorporated itself so firmly into the political structure of Russia that even those who had opposed the establishment of a representative system did not dare to admit it openly for fear of violently shocking public opinion. Having acquired the right to participate in the elaboration of laws, the conservative parties were as anxious as the other parties to retain this right, and as ready to defend it.

Although the Duma had lost a great measure of the confidence of the popular masses since the electoral reform introduced by Stolypin, on the other hand it had greatly strengthened its bonds with the educated classes, the majority of the military cadres, and even the bureaucracy. A great transformation was under way in the political life of the Empire and in the economic and cultural domains as well.

Since the Russo-Japanese war and the disturbances of 1905–1906 the country had achieved a very considerable economic progress. The volume of transactions was steadily growing. The balance of foreign commerce showed a surplus of exports. The railroad network was expanding, and rail transportation and revenues increased steadily. Factory production soared in an unprecedented manner as Russia entered what was clearly a period of industrialization. Consumer statistics and total deposits in savings institutions evidenced steady growth. Peasants' cooperatives experienced a tremendous upward surge. Public finances were well balanced and stood on a firm base. Money—the ruble—had for about twenty years been freely convertible into gold.

Public education and the general level of culture also advanced in giant strides. Elementary schools increased greatly in number and were expected to satisfy the needs of all the children in the country by 1922. Secondary and higher educa-

tion was expanding all the time. The rapidly increasing number of educated persons experienced no difficulty in obtaining
employment with the country in full economic progress.

In the social sphere the situation was more complex. On
one hand, there were still some reasons for even greater worry
than before; on the other, some heartening signs had appeared
which might herald a new social equilibrium. On balance, the
economic life of the peasants appeared to be undergoing slow
but certain progress; their standard of living tended to rise,
and larger parts of the great landowners' estates were steadily
passing into their hands. Stolypin's agrarian reform had been
introduced with the aim of transforming most of the peasants
into small landowners and making them partisans of individual property. It was still far from producing all the expected
results, but some of them had already begun to be visible.

As I said above, all the lands surrounding my estate in the
south of Russia had been acquired by peasants, and I would
have sold mine as well if I had not had excellent relations with
the peasant families who farmed them.

Not counting the lands they rented from landowners, the
peasants in 1917 found themselves masters of three times
more arable land than was held by the owners of large estates.
Yet the number of well-to-do peasants was still relatively
small, and the rural masses still lived very poorly. The rise in
the cultural standard produced the result that material wants
grew more rapidly than resources. As they could not conceive
any other way of improving their condition, the peasants
clung fast to their secular dream of a "big black sharing" and
expected a repartition between them of whatever remained of
the large estates. As to the salaries of the workers, though
they clearly showed an upward movement they were still very
low.

Should the situation of Russia as it presented itself in 1914
have led to pessimistic conclusions, or was there reason for
hope? Would the transformation of the country then in full
progress take on a too-precipitate pace, or would it continue

in an orderly and peaceful manner? The crises, the shocks, and the recriminations which marked the political scene seemed to be the inevitable accompaniment of the profound change taking place. The tide of social discontent was still slowly rising, and had not yet broken in continuous and shifting uncertainties. Would not the millenarian edifice that was the state hold out long enough to be consolidated on the new foundations for reconstruction already being built? The country certainly did not lack worthy, capable, and devoted men to carry out this task, in the administration, in the Duma, and in the *zemstvos*.

In weighing the situation, we had good reason to hope that in spite of the revolutionary tendencies that were surfacing, the country would follow the path of peaceful evolution.

Russia's foreign policy was guided by two principal concerns: first, to assure the support needed to safeguard her national security; second, to defend her interests chiefly on the periphery of the immense empire, and more specially in the Balkans.

During the years I was active in the ranks of Russian diplomacy, the cornerstone of Russian foreign policy was the Franco-Russian Alliance, to which was later added the entente with England. The rapprochement between the St. Petersburg and Paris cabinets was born of Russia's disillusionment over the "Alliance of the Three Emperors." In 1872 the sovereigns of Germany, Austria-Hungary, and Russia had met in Berlin and agreed to act in concert in matters of international policy. Evoking the memory of the Sacred Alliance, they had agreed to fight revolutionary movements that threatened monarchies. In 1873 the three emperors had signed a secret treaty of alliance.

It would seem that a collaboration between three great powers faithful to the traditions of monarchy ought to remain stable, but in fact it did not stand the test of experience. Following the Russo-Turkish war of 1877–1878, the Congress of Berlin deprived Russia of the compensations to which she

felt entitled by virtue of the sacrifices she had made to liberate
Bulgaria from Turkish oppression. The Russian chancellor,
Prince Gorchakov, did not conceal his nation's bitterness at
the indifference displayed by her two allies.

Russia again felt wronged when Germany concluded a
treaty with Austria-Hungary in 1879 and then completed the
alliance in 1882 by the adhesion of Italy. This Triple Alliance, dominated by its most powerful partner, Germany, constituted a menace to its neighbors both east and west, as it
brought the whole center of Europe under German hegemony.

Wishing to avoid a break with Russia, the German chancellor, Prince Otto von Bismarck, offered a "reassurance" in
the form of a new treaty between the emperors of Germany,
Austria-Hungary, and Russia. This treaty was signed in 1881
and renewed in 1884. Each of the three empires promised to
remain neutral if either of the other two was attacked by a
fourth great power. The treaty also contained a reciprocal
pledge to respect the status quo in the Balkans.

When that treaty expired in 1887 it was not renewed, as
Austria and Russia no longer wished to be bound. On the
other hand Bismarck, disturbed by the restoration of military
power in France, was eager to preserve good relations with
St. Petersburg. This induced him to sign with the ambassador
of Russia, and without the knowledge of Austria-Hungary, a
secret accord in Berlin which confirmed—as far as Germany
and Russia were concerned—the main lines of the agreement
of 1884.

The system of "reassurance" conceived by Bismarck made
Germany the guardian of peace and equilibrium between
Vienna and St. Petersburg. By her alliance with Austria-
Hungary Germany engaged herself to render active aid to the
Hapsburg monarchy in case of Russian aggression, and by her
accords with Russia the German Reich promised to stay neu-
tral if the Tsar's Empire was attacked by Austria-Hungary.
Obviously this arrangement was possible only as long as Ger-
man policy had no direct interest in the Balkans and did not

favor Austrian influence there to the detriment of Russian interest.

After he removed Bismarck from leadership in German politics, the young Kaiser Wilhelm II refused to renew the secret Russo-German agreement of 1887, considering that it was not compatible with the Triple Alliance and was too favorable to Russian interests in the Balkans. That was the end of the Russo-German friendship.

It was natural for Russia to turn toward France, who had felt isolated since her defeat by Germany in 1870. The rapprochement with France was recommended—and this may seem strange—by the Russian conservative press (which traditionally had little sympathy for republican France), notably by the periodical published by Katkov who accused Germany and Austria of thwarting Russian policies in the Balkans. Alexander III lent an attentive ear to these assertions.

The Franco-Russian Alliance crystallized little by little. The first conversations between France and Russia led in 1891 to an exchange of memoranda which were limited to recognizing the need for mutual exploration of means for meeting a threat of war directed against either of the two parties. After the particulars of military cooperation were specified, a formal alliance was concluded in 1894. Russia promised to support France by force of arms if the latter were attacked by Germany or by Italy with the support of Germany. France for her part promised to cooperate militarily with Russia if the latter were attacked by Germany or by Austria-Hungary with the support of Germany.

In 1899 Théophile Delcassé, who was then the French minister of foreign affairs, came to St. Petersburg, and it was agreed then that the alliance would remain in force indefinitely unless repealed. The first military convention was signed on August 17, 1892, and was periodically revised by the General Staff chiefs of both nations. During the years preceding the war I was in charge of these documents.

Relations between Russia and England had remained very

cold since the Crimean war. Russian national opinion accused England of having instigated that war, and had been badly hurt by the humiliating peace imposed on Russia at the Congress of Paris in 1856.

This resentment against England was revived and kindled afresh during the Russo-Turkish war when in 1878 the English fleet appeared before Constantinople and robbed Russia of the fruits of her victory over the Sultan's empire. During the years that followed, Russia had collided with England over a great many points: in the Balkans, in Persia, in Afghanistan, in Tibet, in the Far East. The ill will born of conflicting interests was made even worse by the traditional antipathy of the British to the autocratic form of government still in force in Russia.

For her part, England was beginning to feel uneasy at the encroachments on her positions of the new "world politics" (*Weltpolitik*) of Germany. In 1900 Kaiser Wilhelm II decided to endow his country with a powerful high seas fleet. The policy of "splendid isolation" of the "superb Albion" was finally proved indefensible. France also wanted to strengthen her security in Europe and overseas in order to counter the German impetus. In 1904 the cabinets of London and Paris had concluded the "Entente Cordiale." Its principal architects were King Edward VII and Théophile Delcassé.*

With a view to discouraging the aggressive tendencies of the Triple Alliance, Delcassé dreamed of completing the Entente Cordiale with an Anglo-Russian rapprochement. There were many serious obstacles to that. In England as well as in

---

* By virtue of the Entente Cordiale France abandoned Egypt to British influence and England declared that she had no interests in Morocco. Delcassé, who was the French minister of foreign affairs from 1898 to 1905, had succeeded in smoothing out the great difficulties that had erupted between France and England on account of Egypt when Jean Baptiste Marchand's expedition reached the Nile in 1899. In 1901 Delcassé had obtained from the government in Rome a declaration that Italy would not participate in a German war of aggression against France.

Russia public opinion still bore marks of mutual suspicion, and new cause for friction had been added to the old ones.

Following the outburst of xenophobic violence committed in China by the sect known as the Boxers, Russian armed forces had occupied the Chinese province of Manchuria to protect a railway that was under construction to establish communication with Vladivostok and Port Arthur. Russia's two rivals in that area—Japan and England—had taken offense and in 1902 concluded an agreement by which England promised to stay neutral in case of a Russo-Japanese war and to give mliltary aid to Japan if Russia was supported by France. When Japan started the anticipated war two years later, England maintained a rather unfriendly neutral position toward Russia.

Taking advantage of the Russo-Japanese war, Kaiser Wilhelm, who had already started underhand dealings against France in Morocco, now tried to undermine the Franco-Russian Alliance. During a meeting he had with Nicholas II in 1905 at Björkë, in Finnish waters, he took advantage of the Tsar's good faith and induced him to sign a treaty of alliance between the two empires. One clause of this agreement stipulated that France would be informed of the new alliance and would be invited to join it. The Tsar did not realize that the document prepared in Berlin would be incompatible with the Franco-Russian Alliance and would upset the bases of European equilibrium.

It was not until about seven weeks later that Count Lamsdorf, the Russian minister of foreign affairs, learned of the nasty trick played on the Tsar and explained to him that the agreement he had signed without France's knowledge could not be sustained. Emperor Nicholas thereupon hastened to advise Wilhelm II that the accord should be considered null and void.

Izvolskii, who replaced Lamsdorf in 1906, was convinced that two nations, one continental and the other maritime and thus with complementary economies and without common borders, should be able to find some common ground for agreement. He proceeded in the same manner as Delcassé had. Instead of trying to obtain an agreement of a general character, he applied himself to solving the concrete problems that gave rise to the most grievous conflicts between England and Russia by confronting them one after another in a realistic way.

Negotiations led in 1907 to an agreement signed by Izvolskii and British Ambassador Sir Arthur Nicholson.* In Persia the political and economic influences of Russia and England were delineated: the former reserved the northeastern zone and the latter the southeastern; in the intermediate or so-called neutral region, the activities of both powers were to be exercised jointly. Russia recognized the exclusive influence of England in Afghanistan. As to Tibet, England promised to recall her troops from that country and to respect its independence, which Russia also guaranteed.

Though the objectives of the 1907 agreement may seem narrowly restricted, it had consequences of tremendous importance. It completely transformed the atmosphere of Anglo-Russian relations and prepared the ground for a close collaboration between Russia and the British Empire during the First World War. The task accomplished by Izvolskii was greatly facilitated by the presence at the head of the British Foreign Office of Sir Edward Grey, and by the intelligent and devoted efforts of the excellent Russian ambassador in London, Count Alexander Benckendorff.

Of all the regions situated on the periphery of the Russian Empire, the Balkan area was the one where Russia's most important interests converged. Russian foreign policy was largely determined by events that unfolded in this frequently troubled zone. Russia sought twin objectives in the Balkans. She wanted to obtain free access to the Mediterranean through the Straits of the Bosporus and the Dardanelles and to protect

* Sir Arthur Nicholson later became Lord Carnock. He was an old friend of my father.

herself against the passage through that waterway of an enemy fleet bent on attacking the Russian coast of the Black Sea. Furthermore, she wanted to guarantee the independent political existence of the Balkan peoples of all faiths who had long been dominated by the Turks, and to safeguard them against any new servitude.

The "Question of the Straits" of Constantinople arose with the advent of Russian power on the shores of the Black Sea, which had been under the exclusive control of the Sultans since the fall of Byzantium.

A predominantly continental country, Russia had always tried to extend her domain toward the open seas. At the end of a long struggle with Turkey, Russia succeeded under Peter the Great in reaching the Black Sea, and under Catherine II in consolidating her position there; but she was obliged to accept the fact that the exit from this sea to the Mediterranean remained in the hands of her ancient enemy. As the Bosporus and the Dardanelles were part of the territorial waters of Turkey, the passage of ships through these Straits required the consent of the Sublime Porte.* Since the weakening of the Ottoman Empire and the installation of a great power on the shores of the Black Sea, the Sultan's government had to agree that regulation of navigation through the Straits was to be governed by international agreement. The fact that the Bosporus and the Dardanelles divided Turkey's European possessions from her Asian territories and that her capital, Constantinople, was on the shores of the Bosporus enabled the Porte to refuse passage to foreign ships under conditions that would expose its control of the Straits to any danger—and the Porte was especially wary of foreign warships in its waters. Fearing Russia above all others, Turkey was particularly disinclined to admit warships flying the Russian flag. The Empire of the Tsars, on the other hand, as the power most interested in the Question of the Straits, obviously sought to obtain from

* The old designation of the Turkish (or Ottoman) government during the time of the Sultans.

the Porte the arrangement that would best suit Russian interests.

The peace treaty of Kuchuk Kainarji, completed in 1774, was the first of a long series of conventions relative to passage through the Straits. This pact, the fruit of a victory, guaranteed to Russia possession of the north coast of the Black Sea and accorded to Russian merchant vessels free passage from that sea.

Invoking an "ancient rule of the Ottoman Empire," Turkey had always, quite logically, attempted to prevent passage of warships of any country through the Straits in times of peace. During periods when Turkey might be at war, she reserved the right, in the interest of her own defense, to allow the fleets of her allies to pass into the Black Sea (it would hardly have been possible to deny her this right in view of her sovereignty over the Straits). Obviously it would be in the interests of the Ottoman government, if at war with Russia, to allow warships hostile to the Empire of the Tsars to enter the Black Sea. Only an alliance with Turkey could protect Russia from such a risk, but a lasting collaboration between these two countries was practically impossible: too many differences divided them.

Throughout history there were only three attempts to put such an alliance into practice. These arose from exceptional circumstances and lasted briefly. During the French Revolution and the Napoleonic wars Russia and Turkey concluded two alliances against France, but both were short-lived.* Then in 1833, Sultan Mamud II, seeing his throne seriously threatened by the revolt of Mohammed Ali, the pasha of Egypt, requested the aid of the Russian Emperor Nicholas I. The two sovereigns concluded a defensive alliance at Hunkyar Iskelesi, the price of which was that the Sultan promised "to close the

* The alliance treaties of 1793 and 1805 between Russia and Turkey gave Russia the right to use the Straits for passage of warships. The treaty of 1805, moreover, engaged Turkey to close the Straits to all armed vessels except those of Russia and, of course, those of Turkey. These treaties were ephemeral: a war between the two countries broke out in 1806.

Straits and to permit no foreign warship to enter under any pretext," be it in time of war or time of peace. This was tantamount to making Turkey Russia's guardian of the Black Sea. Such an arrangement clearly offered too many advantages to Russia to be acceptable to the great maritime powers. Great Britain and France made remonstrances so menacing to the Porte that when the treaty of Hunkyar Iskelisi expired in 1841 the government of St. Petersburg agreed to sign a Straits convention that same year with Turkey, France, England, Austria, and Prussia, since it would be impossible to renew the previous treaty.

The 1841 convention confirmed the old rule that the Straits would be closed [to foreign warships] when the Porte was at peace. Turkey recovered her freedom to allow foreign warships to pass through the Straits in case of a war in which she was engaged. The regulation of the Straits of Constantinople became a European question, no longer simply a Russo-Turkish one, and the prohibition of passage for warships through the Straits in time of peace became a prescription of European public law. This was the consecration of the Turkish thesis.

The stipulations of the convention of 1841 remained in force until 1914. They were confirmed by the Treaty of Paris in 1856. That instrument, built upon Russian defeat in the Crimean war, also imposed on Russia the neutralization of the Black Sea by stating that this body of water would be "forbidden to all warships be they of riparian powers (of the Black Sea) or of any other power." When Prince Alexander M. Gorchakov, the Russian chancellor, took advantage of the Franco-Prussian war to declare that Russia would no longer accept such a humiliating blow to her sovereignty, an *ad hoc* conference held in London in 1871 revoked the neutralization of the Black Sea. The Berlin treaty of 1878 ratified once again the terms of the 1841 convention.

Ever since the treaty of Kuchuk Kainarji in 1774, Russia, for want of something better, had accepted the solution proposed by Turkey. Indeed, the rule obliging Turkey to forbid entrance to non-Turkish warships in time of peace had presented certain advantages for Russia by making a sudden attack on the Russian coast more difficult. It was only much later that Russia began to think of the interests that might be served by free exit of her warships from the Black Sea to the Mediterranean and vice versa. During the Russo-Japanese war, the Russian government would have been happy to reinforce the squadrons which it sent to the Pacific in 1904 by the addition of naval forces from the Black Sea, and its effort was damaged by its being unable to do so. Turkey was free to increase her forces rapidly by acquiring warships from abroad (thus in January 1914, Turkey purchased from Germany two battle cruisers, the *Breslau* and the *Goeben*). Russia, on the other hand, was deprived of the possibility of similarly assuring the defense of her southern coast because no warships from other waters could be introduced into the Black Sea, whether they be from foreign or Russian shipyards or from Russian fleets in other seas.

When Alexander P. Izvolskii, a man of energy and ambition, replaced Count Lamsdorf in the Ministry of Foreign Affairs, he attempted to have the statute governing the Straits modified in Russia's favor. In course of the negotiations which he began in 1907 with Sir Edward Grey for a rapprochement between Russia and Great Britain, Izvolskii suggested that the Straits Question be included in their discussion. The Russian minister brought out the fact that the projected entente would be especially appreciated in Russia if it led to free access to the Mediterranean for Russia's Black Sea fleet; on the other hand, Russia would prefer to forego this privilege if it appeared it would entail opening the Black Sea to warships of nonriparian powers. The English minister evinced a willingness to examine Russian aspirations on this point, which the Russian side saw as great progress. But Sir Edward Grey pointed out that English opinion would not understand how the Straits could be opened to the Russian fleet without also being opened to the English fleet, and consideration of the subject was abandoned.

In 1908, when the Hapsburg monarchy annexed the Turkish provinces of Bosnia and Herzegovina, which it had occupied since the Berlin treaty of 1878, Izvolskii suggested in a conversation with his Austrian colleague, Baron Alois Lexa von Aehrenthal, that in exchange for Russian consent to a revision of that treaty Austria-Hungary should, when the time came, support Russian aspirations for free passage through the Straits of warships belonging to countries bordering the Black Sea. Austria proclaimed the annexation of the two provinces but failed to give Russia the requested support. Izvolskii's efforts were to no avail.

In a secret memorandum that I wrote early in 1914 for the Tsar and the interested ministers, I summed up the position of Russia concerning the problem of the Straits under Turkish control as follows: *

> The European powers will not be willing to open the Straits solely to the powers bordering the Black Sea, as we had for a time thought. Even supposing that there exists a possibility that an opening of the Straits could be achieved by means of diplomatic negotiation, we would have to accept free passage through these waters for warships of all nations.** This kind of modification of the present Straits re-

* In the papers of Mr. de Basily, which Mrs. Lascelle de Basily has donated to the Hoover Institution, is a lithographed copy of a memorandum *On Our Goals in Regard to the Straits,* dated November 1914, prepared and signed by Basily. This summation seems to be another version of the memorandum mentioned above as prepared "early in 1914." Memoranda forwarded to the Emperor and the ministers certainly would be typewritten and not lithographed. Hence it seems obvious that the November edition is an elaboration of the earlier memorandum. The exact wording given here could not be found in the lithographed memorandum. However, the same message is repeated in essence in the lithographed edition which appears for the first time in English translation at the end of this volume. See Appendix I. (Editor's note.)
** Here I made allusion to Izvolskii's endeavors.

gime would be contrary to our traditional point of view, namely, that—inasmuch as the Straits are not under our control—our strategic interests must oppose the admission of any foreign naval force into the Black Sea, and that the closure of the Straits favors us in that it deprives powers hostile to us of the possibility of preparing an aggression against us in the Black Sea during peacetime.

Recently there have been some objections presented against this thesis and it has been alleged that the closure of the Straits presents more disadvantages than advantages for us. Indeed, the closure of the Straits does not protect us against wartime penetration into the Black Sea by an enemy fleet if such an operation be realized through cooperation with Turkey. Moreover, the closure gives us a false security by causing us to believe that Turkey is the only adversary with whom we must reckon in the Black Sea.

Turkish domination of the Straits presented inconveniences for Russia not only from the strategic standpoint but in the economic sphere as well. On several occasions Turkey had interrupted the free passage through the Straits of merchant vessels en route to and from Russian ports. Without going into the too-distant past, one can recall that this was done during the Greco-Turkish war of 1897 and during the Italo-Turkish war in 1911–1912, not to mention the years of the First World War, when Turkey was aligned on the side of the enemies of Russia. Figures for the decade 1903–1912 show that 37 per cent (in terms of net value) of Russian exports were transported via the Dardanelles.* A commercial artery of such importance to Russia could not be blocked without causing serious damage.

Neutralization had been considered as one means to obviate the inconveniences resulting from Turkish sovereignty over the Straits. All powers would be bound by an international

---

* During this period Russia exported large quantities of wheat and raw materials through the Black Sea. One must also keep in mind that the south of Russia was Russia's richest region.

treaty to respect free passage through that waterway for all merchant and military vessels, in time of war as well as in time of peace; further, all military action would be forbidden in the zone of the Straits, and all fortifications there would be destroyed. One advantage of neutralization was that it could be applied without modifying the territorial status quo in the Straits region. But the idea of neutralization, in spite of all its apparent first attractions, was discarded by the Russian experts each time they had occasion to study it closely. It was pointed out that in the modern world legal prescriptions have value in international relations only when they are effectively supported by force. Demilitarization would only render more possible a surprise attack by a state desirous of seizing the Straits or mounting an attack against Russia. The threat of such an eventuality would even oblige Russia to occupy the Straits in case of international complications to prevent them from falling into enemy hands. The creation of an international force for the defense of the Straits would be of no use if the powers [constituting that force] came to be divided, and indeed it would be in just such a case that these troops would be called upon to act.

In spite of all the inconveniences that Turkish sovereignty over the Straits caused for Russia, the continued possession of that waterway by Turkey was long considered a relatively satisfactory solution from the Russian point of view. It was pointed out that Turkey was not strong enough to stand up to Russia and was therefore obliged to consider Russian interests. In addition, Turkish control of the Bosporus and the Dardanelles freed Russia from concern over their defense as well as from the responsibility for administration of the zone, which obviously would be incumbent on Russia if she were to take possession.

This view of the question ceased to be plausible, however, if Turkey were to become the tool of a strong power other than Russia or if she were to associate herself with powers hostile to Russia. It would be even less acceptable to Russia if

Turkey were to be ejected from the zone of the Straits by another state. It logically followed that Russia would never allow a great power to establish control over the artery and thus acquire a powerful weapon against her. As early as 1829, Count Karl Nesselrode, the Russian chancellor, had expressed the idea that if such a case were to present itself, "the Russian government will be obliged to take the most energetic measures to see that the entrance of the Black Sea does not fall into the hands of any great power whatsoever."

At the end of 1913 there were reasons to fear that new and powerful hands were about to seize control of the Straits, and that Russia, following the recommendations of Count Nesselrode, would have to oppose them by force. Since his accession, Wilhelm II of Germany had turned his gaze toward the Near East and tried to foment German penetration in Turkey. German instructors had given aid to the Turkish army and contributed to its victory over the Greeks in 1897. In 1898 the Kaiser visited Sultan Abd-ul-Hamid and in a speech at Damascus declared himself to be the friend of the Sultan and of the Moslems. In 1902, a German company obtained the concession for construction of a railroad from Constantinople to Baghdad.

In 1913, at the request of the Turks, a German military mission was sent to Turkey to reorganize the army; its leader, General Liman von Sanders, was named commander of the Turkish army corps stationed at Constantinople. This act was equivalent to giving Germany a preponderant position at Constantinople and over the Straits. The government and Russian opinion saw it as a threat to Russian interests and were acutely disturbed.

On January 13, 1914, Kokovtsov, the president of the Russian Council of Ministers, Sazonov, the minister of foreign affairs, and the supreme military authorities met in St. Petersburg to examine the situation and consider the measures to be taken. Paramount in this discussion was the desire to avoid a rupture of relations with Germany. Kokovtsov stated that he would consider a war with Germany at that time the greatest disaster for Russia. Sazonov expressed the same thought, and it was decided to continue conversations with Germany while avoiding any aggravation of relations with that power. Germany agreed to a superficial concession: General Liman von Sanders was promoted to the rank of Turkish marshal and charged with the duties of inspector-general of the Turkish army, while the troops in the Constantinople zone were placed under the command of a Turkish general. Russia, anxious not to aggravate the situation, contented herself with a solution that was no more than an appearance and thus gave clear proof of her peaceful intentions. The Liman von Sanders mission, on the other hand, certainly helped to pave the way for a German-Turkish alliance against Russia and thus for halting Russian communications through the Straits, two contingencies which became realities six months later when the war of 1914 broke out.

When that catastrophe occurred, people in Russia thought the time had finally come to resolve the Question of the Straits. Possession of the Bosporus and the Dardanelles had never ceased to be the secular dream of Russia. This ambition seemed as natural as wanting to have the keys to one's own house. Sentiment as well as practical interest lay behind the ambition, for those of Christian Orthodox religion had always nurtured the hope that Constantinople, the birthplace of their faith, would one day be liberated from Moslem domination and that the cross would replace the crescent on the ancient Cathedral of Santa Sophia. Neither public opinion nor even governmental circles doubted that one day these aspirations would be realized. However, when faced with the risks of international magnitude that could result from a Russian expedition against the Straits, the government of the Tsar had always treated this subject rather academically and had not applied itself to methodical advance preparation of the military and naval means necessary for the execution of a raid into the Bosporus zone. This is one of the reasons why Rus-

sia was unable to carry out such an operation during the First
World War.

If Russia had been able to prevent the closing of the Straits
during that war, either through force or, even better, through
an entente with Turkey, events would have taken another
course. The Russian army would have received arms and mu-
nitions through the Straits, the country would not have been
economically isolated, the war would not have lasted so long
and its outcome would, perhaps, have been more favorable for
Russia.

—4—

Crisis and War

At times I had occasion to take automobile rides with my friend Prince Franz von Hohenlohe, the Austro-Hungarian military attaché in St. Petersburg. I occupied at that time the post of vice-director of the Chancellery of the Ministry of Foreign Affairs and was one of the close collaborators of Minister Sazonov.

One evening in July 1914, we left our respective offices, Hohenlohe the Austro-Hungarian embassy and I the Ministry of Foreign Affairs, and took the road out of St. Petersburg toward Finland. The huge forests of black pine were immersed in absolute silence, undisturbed by the slightest breath of air. It was the time of the marvelous white nights of the northern summer. The sun had scarcely disappeared beneath the horizon only to rise again about an hour later. A faint, pale light illumined the landscape, sad and austere, and increased in us a certain state of anxiety inspired by the recent political news.

The Archduke Franz Ferdinand, heir to the crown of Austria, had been assassinated on June 28 at Sarajevo. In spite of the denials of the government at Belgrade, the Austro-Hungarian Empire held the Serbian leaders responsible for having instigated this political crime, and threatened to crush Serbia. The Russian people, faithful to the ties of blood that united them with this Slavic nation, raised their voices against the Hapsburg design to humiliate their Serbian brothers.

Franz von Hohenlohe and I could not turn our thoughts from the tension growing day by day between our two countries. We could already foresee some of the possible consequences of the Sarajevo murder. Taking me by the arm, Hohenlohe said, "Do you understand that you cannot go to war? If you do, you will expose yourself to revolution and to the ruin of your power." I replied to my friend that while some changes within Russia and perhaps even a serious internal crisis were probable in the future, at present there was no indication of internal trouble. Public opinion was clamoring for an intervention in support of Serbia, and the Russian government would have the approval of the entire nation if it judged itself obliged to act. I added forcefully, "You commit a serious error of calculation in supposing that fear of a revolution will prevent Russia from fulfilling its national duty now. As for the future, who can predict that with certainty?"

Knowing Hohenlohe, I could not doubt his sincerity. Had Austria and Germany not allowed themselves to be swept into the European crisis in the beginning by the illusion that Russia would finally yield before their threats of war? This fatal illusion helped greatly to precipitate the catastrophe.

Russia most definitely did not want war.

Several days later, on July 23, 1914, Raymond Poincaré, the president of the French Republic, terminated a visit in Russia and embarked for France. After having attended his departure from Kronstadt, I returned to St. Petersburg on the Admiralty yacht carrying the ministers. It chanced that I spent the time of our crossing, about an hour, in a cabin with General Sukhomlinov, the minister of war. Of course we spoke of the international tension.

I asked the general what our military situation was in case we were forced to enter into war. The minister presented a long, detailed exposition of our military preparedness, making it plain that I was to convey this information to my chief, Sazonov. General Sukhomlinov first outlined for me a tableau of the vast program undertaken since 1913 by Germany for the reinforcement of its army. He particularly emphasized Germany's superiority in terms of artillery, especially heavy artillery: "At present," he told me, "every German division is provided with fourteen batteries, while our divisions have only seven. As you know, two months ago we had to adopt a plan to increase our military potential in order to counter these German measures. In the interests of our security we had hoped that the projected effort might be more ambitious, but we were limited by budgetary considerations. It was decided to augment our peacetime troop strength by one-third. We should add 13,000 men to our officer corps. The number of batteries and artillery pieces assigned to each of our divisions will be raised to a figure near, if not equal, to the number available to German divisions at present. Unfortunately, this program cannot be completed until 1917, and its fulfillment would necessarily be hindered if war should break out now." The minister of war concluded, "In these conditions, even with the support of France we would find ourselves until 1917, and perhaps even until 1918, in a position of indisputable inferiority with respect to the combined forces of Germany and Austria. Consequently, we should do everything in our power to avoid war."

If the Army leaders recognized the insufficiency of Russian land forces to contend with the Central Powers, the Admiralty command was no less concerned by the relative weakness of our means of action at sea. In the Baltic we had four large battleships under construction but far from completion. Despite all haste taken to finish them during the war, they could not be added to the fleet till the summer of 1915. Until that time the defense of our Baltic shores and of the Gulf of Finland would not be effectively assured. The situation was the same in the Black Sea.

We had serious reason to believe that Turkey and Bulgaria, which were already almost completely under the influence of Berlin, would ally themselves with Germany and Austria in case of armed conflict. Germany had exercised a controlling hand in Turkey ever since the Liman von Sanders mission was installed at Constantinople in November 1913. Turkey was hastily increasing her naval forces, buying ships even from South America.

In view of these disturbing circumstances, it was the duty of the Russian government to take measures to prepare for any eventuality. Recommendations to this end were submitted for the Emperor's approval on February 21, 1914, at the close of a meeting chaired by the minister of foreign affairs and attended by the principal military and naval authorities. Since I had written and signed the memorandum that had been the basis of discussion at this meeting, I was asked to attend and to write the minutes and conclusions. It was decided that the construction of two battleships in the yards at Sebastopol would be accelerated so that they would be completed in the second half of 1915. A third battleship and two cruisers were to be launched during 1916. Further steps were to be taken to increase the transport fleet in the Black Sea and to reinforce and expand the railway network in the Caucasus.

The objective of these arrangements was as much to permit an eventual operation against the Straits at Constantinople as to assure the defense of the coasts of southern Russia. In the hypothesis of a European war—a hypothesis which the aggressive policies of Germany made it impossible for us to overlook—the Straits would become the major, if not the only, link between Russia and the outside world, since egress from the Baltic Sea could easily be prohibited by Germany. Thus the vital interests of Russia made it obligatory to take the necessary precautions to assure free passage through the Straits lest this highly important line of communication also be cut. The First World War clearly demonstrated how much a hostile control of the Straits could damage Russia by exposing her to perilous isolation, and also how much Russia was justified in desiring to establish firm foundations for secure communications through the Straits. To show how important for Russia unrestricted use of the Straits was, we have only to recall that 37 per cent of the net value of all exports from this empire of 180 million people passed through the Straits. When they were closed during the Italo-Turkish war in 1912, the Russian economy suffered considerable damage.

Russia has been accused of having provoked the world war to accomplish her age-old aspirations in the Straits, and the resolutions of the February 21, 1914, meeting have been cited as proof that Russia planned this war. To refute this insidious assertion one has only to point out the fact, as shown in the minutes of that meeting, that the naval and other measures that were planned on that occasion required several years for completion, and that in consequence Russia could not have been considered ready to attack Turkey five months later. If these minutes mention the possibility of a European war, they envision only a conflict provoked without Russian consent, one imposed in spite of Russian desires. It is only in case of such a conflict that the minutes foresee the possibility of Russian military action against the Straits. Sazonov stated this quite clearly at the meeting in question. We must applaud the clairvoyance and patriotism of the Russian statesman who realized that Russia, in spite of her devotion to peace and her lack of preparation, might soon be drawn into a European conflict, and who worked to prepare her insofar as possible for the serious dangers which would surely come with such a conflagration.

If there can be any doubt concerning Russia's peaceful intentions, then, one need only to consider that Russia's leaders were aware that their military preparedness was insufficient. As the war proved, these apprehensions were well-founded.

It has been asserted that Russia willfully precipitated the catastrophe of the First World War by cancelling the order for partial mobilization on the night of July 30, 1914, and replacing it with an order for general mobilization. This thesis has already been refuted by authors more competent than I in military matters. However, personal recollection enables me to add some testimony to counter these unjustified accusations. On July 23, 1914, the government of Vienna had sent to Serbia an ultimatum whose demands, if accepted, would have amounted to an abandonment of Serbian independence. The Russian minister of foreign affairs, Sazonov, had offered the Vienna cabinet "a frank and straightforward explication" between the Russian and Austrian governments with a view to safeguarding the peace. Austria responded that she would refuse any discussion concerning the ultimatum to Serbia. At the same time, the Viennese government mobilized eight army corps, including one on the Russian border. Then, on July 28, it declared war on Serbia, commencing hostilities immediately with a bombardment of Belgrade.*

Resisting the discouragement caused by the intransigence of Austria and the support given to that power by Germany, Russia relentlessly pursued her efforts at conciliation and tried up to the last moment to avoid a European conflagration. She accepted with profound satisfaction the proposal of Sir Edward Grey, foreign secretary of Great Britain, for submitting the Austro-Russian conflict for mediation at a conference in London at which the four least interested great powers—England, France, Germany, and Italy—would participate. This excellent offer, made on July 25, was rejected on July 27 by the Berlin cabinet and on July 28 by the Vienna cabinet. In the meantime, Sazonov proposed to the Austro-Hungarian ambassador in St. Petersburg that England and Italy be charged with mediation of the conflict. On July 29 this suggestion was rejected.

Confronted by the increasingly unyielding attitude of the Central Powers and the Austrian aggression against Serbia, Russia was forced to realize that the chances of a peaceful solution were becoming more and more slight. Russia could

* The news of this bombardment was made known in St. Petersburg on the afternoon of July 29.

not abandon little Serbia to the violence of the powerful empire of the Hapsburgs: that would be cowardice. She could
not capitulate before the Austro-German thrust in the Balkans. That would have been more than a humiliation: it
would have been the acceptance of Germanic hegemony in
Europe. For two hundred years European diplomacy had
recognized that no radical change of balance in the Balkans
could be realized without an accord between Austria and
Russia, and that at the risk of putting torch to gunpowder.

It cannot be sufficiently stressed that on account of Russia's size and the relative weakness of her means of transport, mobilization and concentration of the Russian Army demanded much more time than was required by the Austrian
and German armies. It was therefore vital that Russia not let
herself fall too far behind the Central Powers in this regard.
The question was, would Russia respond to the Austrian
provocation by a partial mobilization or by a general mobilization of her army?

For the same reasons that caused the slowness of Russia's
mobilization, her technical mechanism for mobilization had
been established in such a way that if only a part of the Army
were put on war footing it would no longer be·possible to
apply the general mobilization plan. It was well known that
the ties of alliance between Austria and Germany made it
impossible to consider an armed conflict with the former
country without the automatic intervention of the latter. In
these conditions, it would have been folly for Russia to opt
for a partial mobilization and thus risk confronting a German mobilization with only a dismembered military machine.

Having been shown the dangers of a partial mobilization
by the General Staff, the sovereign made up his mind to
order a general mobilization on the evening of July 29.

Sazonov charged me with relating this decision to the
French ambassador, Maurice Paléologue. I explained to him
the imperious reasons that militated against a partial mobilization. Since the order for the general mobilization would

not appear until the next morning, it was important that this decision not be made known to Berlin during the night, that is, before it became public in Russia.* Therefore I was obliged to tell Paléologue, "I know without doubt that your cipher will not furnish all the necessary guarantees of security and that there is every reason to believe your message will be known immediately to the Germans." Paléologue expressed great surprise, but acquiesced to my plea that his communication be sent to Paris in a Russian code of absolute security. My old friend Charles de Chambrun, first secretary of the French embassy, was assigned to accompany me to my office and there, aided by one of my associates, he coded his ambassador's message with the Russian cipher I supplied. He had just finished this task when Sazonov received a telephone call from Peterhof Palace. The Emperor told him that he had decided to suspend the general mobilization and to order the mobilization of only thirteen Army corps stationed in the Kiev, Odessa, Moscow, and Kazan military districts. It was about eleven o'clock in the evening. Paléologue's telegram, which had not yet been sent, was immediately changed to conform to the new orders.

This change of decision was motivated by a telegram the Tsar had just received from Kaiser Wilhelm II, in which the German ruler made it known that he was using "all his powers to promote a direct understanding between Russia and Austria."

Germany had given firm support to Austria since the beginning of the crisis, and had rejected all of Sazonov's attempts at conciliation. In the afternoon of July 29, Count

* The version of this conversation given by Paléologue in *An Ambassador's Memoirs,* London, F. A. Holt, 1923–1925 (3 volumes), vol. 1, pp. 42–43, is not entirely accurate. Paléologue writes that I told him that the Russian government had decided "secretly to commence general mobilization." A general mobilization obviously cannot be kept secret, even for a very short time; all we could hope for was that the news of our mobilization would not be known by the German government before it had been made public in Russia the next day (July 30).

Friedrich von Pourtalès, German ambassador in St. Petersburg, had even stated to Sazonov that Germany would mobilize unless Russia stopped her military preparations. This stance was even more unjustified in view of the fact that at that time Russia had not even ordered the mobilization for her covering troops against Austria, while Austria had already put eight army corps on war footing and was proceeding with important military measures on the Russian front. The telegram from the Kaiser, which we have just mentioned, was written in a tone that contrasted singularly with the statement of Count von Pourtalès. Nicholas II believed he saw in it an indication of Germany's return to more peaceful feelings. Clinging to this hope, he answered the German Emperor immediately, thanking him for his "conciliatory and amicable" telegram and proposing that the dispute be submitted to the Hague tribunal. The Tsar's telegram was sent at 8:20 that evening. Now more confident of the future, Nicholas II took immediate steps to replace the general mobilization with a partial mobilization, as explained above.

But the hopes that had been rekindled in the heart of the Tsar were short-lived. On that same night of July 29–30, at one o'clock in the morning, Kaiser Wilhelm telegraphed the Tsar, this time in an almost menacing tone, that his earlier message should not be interpreted in a sense different from that of the statement made in the afternoon by Count von Pourtalès. As for the Tsar's proposal of arbitration, the Kaiser let it drop without even a word of response. The telegram sent by Emperor Nicholas at 8:20 in the evening—containing the very important proposal for submitting the conflict to the Hague tribunal—was not published in the German White Paper on the origins of the war, which however contained all the other telegrams exchanged between the two emperors between July 24 and August 2. Moreover, in that publication the German Chancellery abridged the text of the Kaiser's telegram of 1:00 a.m. by omitting the first lines, in which Kaiser Wilhelm acknowledged receipt of the Tsar's tele-

gram. Germany obviously wanted to cover up the offer made
by the Tsar as well as Kaiser Wilhelm's rejection. The complete texts of these telegrams were published at my instiga-
tion in Russia in 1915, on the occasion of the publication
of a translation of the German White Paper.

The news received on July 30 in St. Petersburg added to
the state of anxiety there: Germany was activating its military preparations while Austria was expecting a general
mobilization order. At 1:00 p.m. a telegram from the Russian press agency in Berlin announced that the Berlin *Local
Anzeiger* had just published the news of the general mobilization of the German army. We learned later in the day that
the news given by this semi-official German paper was inac-
curate. The *Kriegsgefahrzustand* [the period of imminent
danger of war], which allows calling up the reserves and is in
effect the equivalent of general mobilization, was not officially
decreed in Berlin until the next day, July 31. Nevertheless,
according to irrefutable information, Germany was already in
full preparation for war on July 30.*

In the early hours of that same afternoon, Sazonov was
called to a meeting of the General Staff. He had just finished a
hasty lunch with Krivoshein, the minister of agriculture, and
myself. Sazonov took me with him. In silence we walked
across the great square of the Winter Palace. Sukhomlinov,
the minister of war, and General Ianushkevich, the chief of
the General Staff, declared to Sazonov that, now that Germany seemed decided to make war, Russia was exposing herself to the greatest peril in failing to go beyond a partial
mobilization that would render her powerless to assemble all
her forces in time to resist the Central Powers. The war could
be lost before it had even begun. The generals would implore

---

* Colonel Gudim-Levkovich, a Russian military attaché then traveling
through Germany, was so struck by the number of troop transports he
saw, especially those carrying reservists, that on that same day, July
30, he asked the Russian ambassador in Berlin to telegraph this information to St. Petersburg.

Sazonov to use all his influence on the Emperor to avert such danger.

While this conference was in progress I waited in a nearby room and chatted with General Iurii Danilov, the quartermaster general. He explained to me how the mechanism for partial mobilization would, from its second day—that is, the day after it went into effect—thwart the execution of a general mobilization, and how consequently the last moment was fast approaching, after which it would no longer be possible to correct the measures taken, especially those concerning transport. Danilov spoke to me clearly and forcibly, as usual. Evidently he wanted me to sum up his explanations for Sazonov without delay in order to make the minister of foreign affairs appreciate for himself the serious consequences that would come with an irrevocable impairment of the mobilization mechanism. As I walked back to the Ministry of Foreign Affairs with my chief, I related to him my conversation with the quartermaster general. Sazanov left immediately for Peterhof, where the Emperor awaited him. After listening to Sazanov, the Tsar capitulated to the arguments of the officers. The order for general mobilization was issued at dawn on July 31. There was no other way out.

Sazonov gives in his memoirs a simple and striking account of the reaction of Emperor Nicholas II, as well as his own state of mind, during the memorable conversation they had that tragic day of July 30, 1914: *

I need not say with what feelings I undertook to fulfill this request, which concerned matters so utterly foreign to me and so organically incompatible with my whole nature and my

* The translation of the following excerpts from Sazonov's memoirs was made from the handwritten original in Russian, which is in the Archives of the Hoover Institution. This original was given by Sazonov to Nicolas de Basily and came to the Institution with the Basily Papers. It has appeared only in English and French translations. These excerpts are from pages 507, 511, 515–516, and 517–518 of the original manuscript. (Editor's note.)

convictions.* Nevertheless I agreed to do what was asked of me, seeing it as a duty I had no right to decline at this moment of terrible responsibility. . . .

I began my report at ten minutes past three and ended at four. . . . The sovereign was silent. Then he spoke in a voice filled with anguish: "This means condemning hundreds of thousands of Russian people to death. Shouldn't one stop short of such a decision?" **

I replied that responsibility for the lives of victims carried away by the war would not rest with him, for he had not wanted this war and both he and his government had done the utmost to avoid it. . . .

Having nothing to add to what I had told the sovereign, I sat opposite him, watching intently as his pale face registered the terrible inner struggle he was going through and mirrored much the same tension I was experiencing. . . . Finally the sovereign said to me—and it seemed that he found it difficult to utter the words—"You are right. There remains for us nothing but to accept the challenge. Transmit my order for mobilization to the chief of the General Staff."

Throughout the day of July 31 Russia, anxious to the last minute to avoid catastrophe, continued her efforts at conciliation with the help of England, in the hope of finding some ground of agreement with Austria. At the same time she sought to assure Germany that the Russian mobilization did not mean war, and in a telegram sent to Kaiser Wilhelm Nicholas II gave his word of honor to that effect.

On August 1, at about 7:00 p.m., I was in Sazonov's office when the arrival of the German ambassador was announced. Count von Pourtalès had come to deliver the declaration of war. We know that Pourtalès was so upset that he allowed two variations to remain in the text of the declaration. I saw Pourtalès leave Sazonov's office. It was a painful sight; tears stood in his eyes. He had believed that Russia would

* Here Sazonov alludes to his own profound religious feelings.
** The French translator omitted this paragraph. (Editor's note.)

allow herself to be intimidated and was prostrate to learn that these calculations had been wrong.

Those ten tragic days from July 23 to August 1 in which the world's destiny was decided remain etched in my memory as a period of horrible nightmare. My close friend Baron Mavrik F. Schilling and I remained at the call of Sazonov during this time and could observe the ever-increasing anguish that tortured him. Our state of mind was similar to that of a man who keeps vigil over a loved one stricken with a grave disease and sees more clearly each day that there is no further hope of saving him from death.*

About twelve years later, after the war had taken its toll in millions of deaths and incalculable suffering and devastation, I happened to meet Gottlieb von Jagow, who had been minister (state secretary) of foreign affairs for the German Empire in 1914. We were dining at Prince Isenburg's home in Berlin. After the meal von Jagow and I retired to a corner of the drawing room and passed in review the tragic events we both had witnessed. It is known that in 1916 Germany repeatedly made offers to conclude a separate peace with Russia. Von Jagow now asked me, "I have never understood why you rejected those offers. Would you please explain to me the reasons?" I answered simply, "We had promised our allies to continue the war at their side. Neither the Emperor nor the imperial government had ever considered betraying Russia's allies in spite of all the dangers presented by the internal situation. After the fall of the tsarist regime, the same attitude of loyalty was adopted without hesitation by the

* At the moment when the threat of war suddenly loomed before us, Count Witte was taking the waters at a German spa. The possibility of a European conflagration was so far from the thoughts of this man who had been Russia's greatest statesman that he was unwilling to believe the alarming news published in the papers. Through a discreet channel he asked us to apprise him of the true situation. I responded through the same channel and in a veiled manner with a telegram stating that I wanted my son who was staying at the seashore in France to return posthaste to Russia. Witte immediately made arrangements to return to St. Petersburg, where he died in 1915.

Provisional Government of 1917, although it was not bound by the agreements concluded by its predecessor. This it did in full cognizance of the fact that it was risking its own existence and that of the newborn democratic regime." Von Jagow responded with astonishment, "That's incredible! Then it was only to be faithful to your engagements that you rejected the life belt we offered you?"

Was this not the same language that the German chancellor Bethmann Hollweg used in 1914 in speaking to Sir Edward Goshen, British ambassador to Berlin, when he treated the guarantee to Belgium as a mere "scrap of paper"?

Through weakness and lack of judgment, the ill-fated Tsar made incalculable mistakes which opened a chasm between himself and his people and precipitated the country into a revolution that was by no means inevitable. If only he had listened to the repeated advice that was given to him during the war, he could have taken advantage of the patriotic spirit to reaffirm his ties with the nation. Nicholas II paid for his faults with the terrible end that befell him and his family, but his memory will always remain innocent of all reproach of disloyalty toward the allies of his country.

The Abdication of Nicholas II

The Interallied Conference in Petrograd came to an end on February 21, 1917, and the foreign delegates departed, certainly anxious about the future of Russia but far from realizing the gravity of the situation.

During the conference General Vasilii Gurko occupied a room in the Hotel d'Europe in Petrograd. One day when I went to see him—it must have been the 19th or 20th of February—our attention was attracted by noise in the streets, and we saw a crowd, largely composed of women, parading on Nevsky Prospect and demonstrating against high prices and the shortage of food. We exchanged remarks expressing our anxiety.

After the close of the Interallied Conference I remained several days in Petrograd, then returned to the Stavka, as the Russians called the General Headquarters. There I found General Mikhail V. Alexeev, who had just returned to Mogilev on March 3. I was most pleased to see him again, but would have been more pleased had he been in better physical condition. He had considered it his duty to return to his functions as chief of staff of the High Command before completely recovering from an illness, and at night he still sometimes suffered attacks of high fever. On March 8, Emperor Nicholas came to Mogilev. As usual, we went to the railway station to await his arrival.

The rush of events had accelerated. Rumors reached us that

strikes had occurred in the big factories of Petrograd, the Putilov metallurgic works. On March 10 we learned through telegrams from the minister of war, Beliaev, and from General Khabalov, commander of the Petrograd Military District, that disorders had broken out in the capital.

The following day, the news was even more alarming. Khabalov informed us that 240,000 workmen had stopped work, that their movement had transformed itself into an uprising rallying to the cry "Down with war!" and that troops had fired on a crowd amassed in Nevsky Prospect.

The disorders had been provoked in Petrograd by a shortage of food supplies, especially of bread. The war had forced the railroads to make an effort beyond their capacity and the result was a growing disorganization of transportation. The inept administration of the minister of the interior, Alexander D. Protopopov, had not been able to resolve the problem of food supply so important in maintaining order in the capital.* This serious fault had been exacerbated by another. At the beginning of the war all regiments of the guard had been sent to the front, and not one unit of well-trained troops was left in Petrograd. On the other hand, a large number of new recruits and reservists—about 160,000 men—had been concentrated in the capital, where they were receiving military instruction. This mass of soldiers, as yet little disciplined, was commanded by reserve officers who were insufficient in number and lacking in necessary authority. Under these conditions the garrison of the capital not only did not constitute an effective guarantee for maintaining order, but could easily become a source of grave danger.

On the morning of March 12 we learned at the Stavka that the troops in Petrograd had refused to use their arms against the crowds, that they had arrested or killed their officers and

* Protopopov, in his typically unconcerned manner, declared that he was certain to be able to contain all disorder with the help of the police, whom he had supplied with machine guns to meet all eventualities.

joined the rebellion. Generals Mikhail A. Beliaev and Sergei S. Khabalov demanded that reliable support troops be sent to Petrograd from the front.

My consternation grew still greater when I learned that in obedience to an order of the Emperor, the president of the Council, Prince Nikolai Golitsyn, had decreed the prorogation of the Duma. There was no longer any doubt in my mind: suddenly we found ourselves faced with a popular uprising. For some time we had known it to be inevitable, but we had not thought it so near at hand, and we dreaded it with our whole being. Yet the Emperor persisted in his blindness and imprudently rejected the support that the Duma would have been happy to give him had he been willing to pay attention to its counsel.

In face of the gravity of the situation, I expressed to General Alexeev my profound conviction that this was the very last opportunity the Emperor would have to rally the opinion of the country—or at least to attempt to do so—and for that it was necessary for him to declare immediately and solemnly his decision to dismiss his incompetent, discredited ministers and to surround himself from then on with collaborators possessing the public confidence. One cannot govern if one has lost the support of both the elite and the masses.

My venerable chief shook his head sadly and showed me a telegram he had received during the night from the president of the Duma, Mikhail Rodzianko. The message was written in anguished terms:

The disturbances are assuming threatening and irreducible proportions. . . . The public authorities have lost all credit and are incapable of pulling the country out of its tragic situation. . . . It is urgent to appoint a government of men who have the confidence of the public. . . . In this terrible hour there is no other solution, and I entreat you to intercede in this sense with His Majesty in order to avoid a catastrophe. Any delay is equivalent to suicide.

General Alexeev added: "This morning I submitted this tele-gram to the Emperor. Again, I did everything possible to con-vince him to take the road to salvation at last. Again, I ran against a wall."

Unwilling to doubt the fidelity of seasoned troops, the Em-peror gave orders that some regiments be taken from the front and dispatched to Petrograd to put down the riots. Would these troops agree to fire against the insurgents? I no longer had many illusions on this subject, and I was convinced that first the mood of the country must be calmed by an assurance that things were going to change. In reality, the morale of the army no longer had the same solidity as before. The ranks of the career officers as well as of the noncommissioned officers had been decimated. The losses had been filled by reservists who were far from presenting the same guarantees of obedi-ence as the cadres of professional military men. The recruits, freshly arrived from their villages, were even less stable. The profound disturbance that had taken hold of people all over the country could not have failed to extend to the Army, where the disappointment caused by military reverses was felt even more deeply than among the civilians. The military shared the discontent of the home front over the economic difficulties of all kinds resulting from the prolongation of the war. Moreover the soldiers, who mostly came from the coun-tryside, expected that their sacrifices would be recompensed by greater consideration for their desire for land, but the pref-erence accorded in high places to the reactionary nobility did not encourage them to hope for a breakup of the large estates.

The obvious incompetence of the ministers chosen by the Emperor tended to convert many officers to liberal, or even radical, ideas. Moreover imprudent speeches pronounced in the Duma against the government had had great repercussions throughout the country and had helped considerably to under-mine the authority of the establishment. Finally, the Army was aroused, as was the rest of the country, by rumors of the con-fidence the sovereigns had placed in the corrupt Rasputin.

What was still worse, they dared—in the Army as well as at the rear—to suspect the Empress of serving the interests of Germany, which in fact was pure calumny. The traditional prestige of the Tsar was too greatly shaken for soldiers already fatigued by war to accept fighting against their brothers in order to defend the tottering authority of the unfortunate sovereign.

So it was not astonishing that during the day of March 12 General Nikolai V. Ruzskii, commander in chief of the Northern Army Group, telegraphed to the Emperor that measures of repression would only aggravate the situation, and that it was a matter of the greatest urgency that the population be calmed and its confidence in him restored.

More and more alarming news arrived at the Stavka. The soldiers were fraternizing with the workmen. The crowd and the insurgent troops were marching to the Duma and expecting it to lead them. Thus contrary to its expectations and its will, the Duma became for a time the center of a movement it was far from having initiated. It was evident to us that, at any price, this moment must be seized to reconstitute power by supporting it on that prestige which the Duma still possessed. The monarchy had yet a chance to be conciliated with the moderate elements. To let this occasion escape was to lose irremediably all control over the development of events and to play into the hands of the parties of the extreme left. Would the liberals who desired an orderly transformation of the country be put aside or even crushed by those for whom progress must begin with the destruction of all the heritage of the past? In short, if the internal struggle were to be prolonged and to spread, the war would necessarily terminate in defeat and failure in our obligations toward our allies. Even should the monarchy accept defeat, the people would not forgive it.

Preoccupied by these somber thoughts, I took advantage of a moment of liberty to visit my friends of the Navy Staff. For years we had had the most confident relations, and our way of looking at things was often the same. These naval officers were cultivated men, liberal and generally well informed, and mostly on an intellectual level superior to that of the Army men. They were in communication by direct wire with the Admiralty in Petrograd and received news from the capital continuously. Since the disturbances of 1905 the Navy had proved particularly vulnerable to revolutionary propaganda. If the agitation won over the fleet, the officers certainly ran the greatest risks of being assassinated. I found my friends most anxious, and as desirous as I to see an eleventh-hour understanding between the monarch and the Duma.

On the evening of this same day, March 12, I dined with the Emperor. The guests were nervous but made an effort not to appear so, and most of the time they chatted about unimportant subjects. They also spoke of the health of the sovereign's daughters and son, who were ill with measles in Tsarskoe Selo. The Emperor, as usual, appeared calm and impassive. He spoke a great deal with his aide-de-camp General Nikolai Ivanov, who sat at his left. About a year earlier, Ivanov, a small man with big white sideburns, had been relieved of his functions as commander in chief of the Southern Army Group. At the beginning of the war he had inflicted a crushing defeat on the Austrians, which had given him a certain prestige. We knew, however, that his successes were due chiefly to the fact that he had then had General Alexeev as his chief of staff. Though not a man of great ability, General Ivanov had a crafty, subtle mind and knew well how to make his way. Since his retirement from command he had been attached to the person of the Emperor and had lived, without doing much of anything, in a special railway carriage at the Mogilev station.

During dinner my table companions explained to me that the sovereign had just appointed Ivanov commander in chief of the Petrograd district, with ample powers to suppress the insurrection, and that he would leave for the capital the next day with the Saint George Battalion, which was stationed at the General Staff Headquarters. This unit was composed of soldiers who had displayed exemplary conduct on the battlefield and had been decorated with the Cross of Saint George.

In 1914 I had had some difference with Ivanov over the clumsy policies practiced in Russian-occupied Galicia. Therefore I was much surprised when, after dinner, he asked me to visit him that same evening in his railway carriage at the station. He gave the same invitation to one of my good friends of the Navy Staff, Captain Bubnov.

When Bubnov and I joined General Ivanov in his railway carriage, he asked us to tell him very frankly what he thought of his mission. We told him that once on the spot he would see whether it was still possible to crush the rebellion with a decisive blow, but that we feared it was already too late. In any case, it seemed to us certain that, in view of the state of mind now prevalent in Russia, there was no chance that the troops could be used against the Duma, and that if the Duma was really at the head of the movement, the expedition was doomed beforehand to failure. We concluded that it would be infinitely preferable to seek some ground of understanding with the Duma and thus separate the relatively moderate elements from the extremist parties. It was necessary at any price to avoid the spread of a civil war with all its disastrous consequences, as well for the monarchy as for the pursuit of the war and the future of the country. The old general replied that he was not far from sharing our point of view. I thought it my duty to repeat the next morning to General Alexeev what I had just said to Ivanov.

We left General Ivanov toward midnight, and en route to our destination we met an officer who confided to us that he had serious reason to believe that the soldiers of the Saint George Battalion would not fire on the insurgents. And this was an elite unit, thought to be reliable under all circumstances.

I accompanied my friend Bubnov to the offices of the Navy Staff. The chief of staff there, Admiral Russin, had just received a telegram from Petrograd informing him that the troops in ever increasing numbers were joining the insurrection, that anarchy was growing in the city, and that, on the demand of the insurgents, the Duma had formed a provisional committee with the purpose of restoring order in the capital, as far as possible.

While I was returning to my offices at about one o'clock in the morning, two automobiles passed me on Dnieprovskii Prospect, moving at high speed toward the station. I immediatey recognized the imperial limousines. The Emperor, then, had decided to leave the Stavka.

The next morning I had the explanation for the monarch's hurried departure. In the afternoon of March 12 he had made up his mind to rejoin his family in Tsarskoe Selo and to leave the following day, but a telephone conversation he had with the Empress during the evening had caused him to hasten his departure. General Alexeev had implored him not to enter the Petrograd zone, where he risked falling into the hands of the insurgents, and not to leave at such a moment the center of command of his armies, where he remained in communication with the whole empire and would be in a better position to make decisions. The Emperor did not yield to these arguments. He was first of all an excellent husband and a good father. In these moments of anguish he was anxious about his family and desired above all to be with them.

During the morning of March 13, in the offices of General Alexeev, I also learned of the latest messages received by the Emperor, and of the last dispositions taken by him before his departure. In the afternoon of March 12 he had been given a telegram from the president of the Duma, Rodzianko, written in terms still more pressing than the one addressed twelve hours earlier to General Alexeev. Rodzianko told the Tsar that civil war had begun and was spreading, that the government was powerless, that it was urgent that the management of affairs be given to people who enjoyed popularity and that the Duma be reconvened. He ended his appeal with these dramatic words: "The hour has come which will decide your fate and that of our country. Tomorrow it may be too late." Thus

Rodzianko, who had struggled so hard to renovate the Russian monarchical system, was striving to the last hour to save the monarchy and the person of the sovereign.

Rodzianko's telegram was followed several hours later by a message from the president of the Council of Ministers, Nikolai D. Golitsyn. This worthy old dignitary, ineffectual and inexperienced, had also finally concluded that the cabinet was unable to fulfill its task: he implored Nicholas II to dismiss his ministers and to appoint either Prince Georgii Lvov or Rodzianko to form a new ministry. He added that the presence of Protopopov in the government had provoked general exasperation.

That evening the Grand Duke Mikhail, brother of the Emperor, had a conversation by direct wire with General Alexeev and asked him to insist with the Emperor that he follow the advice of Golitsyn immediately. General Alexeev, who had had an attack of fever that night, left his bed to go and plead with the Emperor to yield at last to the wise counsels lavished upon him. To add more weight to his supplications, the good general is said to have gone down on his knees before his sovereign (this detail was told me by one of his officers, to whom the general had described the scene). The Emperor retreated as usual into intransigence. He left Rodzianko's telegram without reply and shortly before his departure from Mogilev telegraphed Golitsyn that under the present conditions he considered any change in the cabinet inadmissible. It was the utmost degree of blindness, and those of us who were informed of this message were filled with despair.

The Emperor's train did not leave the Mogilev station until five o'clock in the morning. He was conferring there with General Ivanov when a telegram from General Khabalov was delivered to him. The commander of the Petrograd Military District informed Nicholas II that he was in no position to execute the instructions received and to restore order in the capital because most of the troops had refused to obey orders and the greater part of the city had fallen into the hands of the insurgents. Obviously, it would be impossible to prevent the repercussions this news would necessarily have on the troops at the front. From then on, the preservation of order and unity in the army, as well as the maintenance of transportation, became the principal preoccupation of General Alexeev. He immediately sent an account of the events to all the commanders of army groups and reminded them of their sacred duty to keep the troops faithful to the oaths they had sworn to Emperor and to country.

The news received during the day of March 13 was of extreme gravity. The revolutionaries had become masters of the whole capital, and no faithful troops remained in Petrograd. Toward evening the struggle ended and the situation in the city became more calm. The Committee of the Duma was striving to induce the disbanded soldiers to return to the barracks in order to get them away from the influence of extreme left agitators and to place them once again under the authority of their officers. The railroads' delegate in the Duma, Alexander A. Bublikov, a moderate man whom I knew well, sent out an ardent appeal to the patriotic sentiments of the railwaymen asking them to do their utmost to reestablish proper operation of the railways.

The situation seemed to be taking a new turn. General Alexeev concluded that he must immediately adapt his action accordingly. During the night of March 13–14, he sent a telegram to General Ivanov at Tsarskoe Selo, where the latter was to arrive in the morning. In this telegram Alexeev expressed hope for an understanding with the Duma and recommended the avoidance of force.

In the meantime, the Navy Staff notified us that the socialists were intensifying their action and that it was to be feared that the workers' organizations would "raise the banner of socialism and crush the Duma."

That prophetic phrase was written by my naval friends on the very same day that the Petrograd Soviet of 1917 was to meet for the first time (during the night of March 13–14, in the palace of the Duma). The Soviet had already appeared during the disturbances of 1905 and set itself up as the center of revolutionary action of the socialist parties, but at that time it was composed only of factory delegates. It was now revived on a wider base with the addition of delegates from the Petrograd regiments, thus becoming the "workers' and soldiers' Soviet." If in the first moment of disorder the masses had turned toward the Duma, it remained evident to us that the latter lacked deep roots in the lower strata of the population. Indeed, had this assembly not become in the eyes of the masses "the Duma of great landowners" since June 1907, when Nicholas II had, on the advice of Stolypin, modified the electoral system? The number of deputies elected by the peasants was at that time arbitrarily reduced in order to prevent them from getting the Duma to accept a division in their favor of the great landed properties still belonging to the nobility. In thus taking sides against the peasants, the Tsar had in one blow undermined the prestige of both the crown and the popular representation. The "professional revolutionaries" grouped within the Soviet—sincere socialists and demagogues alike—found their task greatly facilitated. Were we not now about to pay the price of these errors?

The train carrying General Ivanov and the Saint George Battalion left Mogilev on March 13 toward noon and took the Kiev-Petrograd line passing through Vitebsk, Dno, and Vyritsa. The general arrived safely the following morning in Tsarskoe Selo, but without the battalion, which was prevented by railway workers from proceeding to its destination.*

Not wishing to hinder the movement of the troops, the Emperor decided to set out for Tsarskoe Selo via Orsha, Viazma, and Likhoslav and then take the main Moscow-Petrograd line through Bologoe and Malaia Vychera. As usual the Emperor's journey was ensured, for greater security, by two trains, one following the other. The monarch and his immediate suite oc-

* The general managed to see Empress Alexandra but found himself deprived of all possibility to do anything. His mission ended in failure.

cupied one of the trains; the other, called "the service train," was reserved for various military personnel and civilians who accompanied the sovereign, and for his military escort.

In the evening of March 13 the Stavka lost all contact with the imperial trains, and we were seized with great anxiety for the fate of the Emperor. Our first fear was that he had fallen into the hands of the insurgents. But even if such an eventuality was avoided, misfortune had willed that there was no longer any means of communicating with the Emperor at a time when he alone could make the necessary decisions to put an end to the anarchy.

At last, on the morning of March 14, we were able to locate the imperial trains. They had been able to reach Malaia Vychera but could go no farther, the revolutionaries having blocked the line between there and Petrograd. The Emperor was obliged to turn back through Bologoe to Dno. We thought at first that he was trying to continue his journey to Tsarskoe Selo by another line, but in the afternoon we learned that he was on his way to Pskov, where the headquarters of the Northern Army Group, commanded by General Ruzskii, was installed. Evidently the monarch did not wish to go too far from his family and at the same time desired to be in a big military center provided with all means of communication. Pskov was the nearest place connected by direct telegraph with the General Headquarters in Mogilev, and this fact contributed greatly to the Emperor's decision to go there.

Meanwhile, during the day of March 14, the revolutionary movement spread beyond the capital. Since the day before, work had been stopped in all the Moscow factories. Now, twenty-four hours later, Moscow was in full revolution, with the troops no longer obeying their officers and going over to the rebels. The other large cities also were beginning to give way to the revolutionary fever. We learned that the big naval base at Kronstadt, situated near the capital, had revolted and that the commander of the port had been assassinated. To avoid a general slaughter of the officers, Admiral Adrian I. Nepenin had been obliged to put the Baltic fleet under orders of the Committee of the Duma. In Petrograd, all the ministers had been relieved of their functions by the revolutionaries and the Provisional Committee of the Duma had undertaken the management of the governmental institutions. Rodzianko notified the Stavka of these developments that afternoon. However—as a telegram from Count Kapnist of the Naval Staff emphasized—beside the Duma there loomed the growing menace of the parties of the extreme left grouped around the Soviet of Workers' and Soldiers' Deputies. In order to spread the revolution, these parties had just sent emissaries to the armies. Their arrival on the northern front in the region of Pskov had already been reported.

Under the impress of this news, in the afternoon of March 14 Alexeev, in his fine, regular handwriting, wrote a telegram to the Emperor to put him face to face with his responsibilities. He said, in substance, that the disorganization at the rear would deprive the army of its supplies, that it was not possible to ask it to fight the enemy if a revolution was spreading behind the front; under the conditions prevailing, repression of the unrest by force would present great danger and would lead Russia and the army to their ruin; if the sovereign did not decide immediately to make concessions susceptible of restoring tranquility, power would pass tomorrow to the extremist elements and Russia would suffer all the horrors of revolution.*

General Alexeev's initiative was immediately supported by messages to the Emperor from his first cousin, the Grand Duke Sergei Mikhailovich, general inspector of the artillery, and by General Alexei Brusilov, commander of the Southwestern front.

---

* At first the communications service of the Stavka tried to transmit this telegram to the Emperor in Tsarskoe Selo. When at about three o'clock in the afternoon it became known that Nicholas II was on his way to Pskov, Alexeev's message was immediately sent there.

In order to move the Emperor to make the decision so long awaited, it was necessary to submit to him the text of a declaration which he could sign for publication. Remarking that General Alexeev was tired and ailing, I offered to assist him and proposed writing a draft manifesto and an explanatory telegram to the Emperor. Alexeev asked me to do so, and some time later I brought him the following text:

From one moment to the next, anarchy threatens to spread throughout the country. The disintegration of the Army is becoming an ever more pressing danger. Under these conditions the continuation of the war would no longer be possible. The situation requires the immediate publication of an imperial act that might still be able to restore calm. But this result can be obtained only by the constitution of a responsible ministry whose formation would be entrusted to the president of the Duma. Present intelligence permits us to hope that the members of the Duma, led by Rodzianko, are still capable of halting the general collapse, and that it will be possible to work with them. Each hour that is lost, however, diminishes the chances of maintaining and reestablishing order and facilitates a seizure of power by extreme left elements. For this reason, I beg Your Imperial Majesty to authorize immediate publication by General Headquarters of the following manifesto:

We declare the following to all our faithful subjects. The ferocious and powerful enemy is gathering his last forces for the struggle against our fatherland. The decisive hour approaches. The destiny of Russia, the honor of our heroic Army, the well-being of the people, all the future of our dear fatherland demand that at any price the war be pursued to a victorious end. Wishing to solidify all the forces of the nation in order to hasten the victory, I consider it my duty to appoint a ministry responsible to the representatives of the people, and to entrust the president of the Duma, Rodzianko, to form it with the help of persons possessing the confidence of all Russia.

I firmly hope that all the faithful sons of Russia will unite closely around the throne and the national representation, and will give to our valiant Army their fervent support for the

achievement of its glorious task. In the name of our beloved country, I appeal to all Russians to fulfill their sacred duty toward Russia, in order to prove once again that she remains as firm as ever, and that no effort of her enemies can destroy her.
May God help us.

Alexeev showed this text to General Lukomskii, the quartermaster general, who made two minor word alterations, and the telegram was dispatched on March 14 at ten o'clock in the evening to Pskov, where Nicholas II had arrived at seven o'clock in the evening.

This telegram proposed changes much more profound than those which had been contemplated until then. In fact, only a few days before—outside the extremist parties—it had been generally accepted that in order to redress the situation it would suffice for the Emperor to call into the government men known for their honor and their liberal ideas, without however renouncing the right of choosing his ministers. An intimate collaboration between the government and the national representation had seemed clearly indispensable, but that did not necessarily imply the responsibility of the cabinet before the chamber, that is to say a parliamentary system, which Russia did not seem to be in condition to adopt before a period of political apprenticeship. But again the Emperor had delayed too long and now, to recover lost time, it was in all evidence necessary to go ahead with concessions. Moreover, the text proposed to the Emperor contemplated that the cabinet would thenceforth be placed under the control of the Duma.*

Alas, events had gone so fast that even this concession, however important it seemed to us at that moment, could no longer suffice to calm the minds of the people. The excitement of the crowd had taken on such proportions that only sweeping measures could appease it. We did not have to wait long to see this confirmed.

* Such a solution had been recommended by the elective members of the State Council in a telegram to the Emperor on March 13.

During that night of March 14–15 all our attention was turned toward Pskov, where the Emperor was. At a very late hour, General Ruzskii had a long conversation by direct wire with the president of the Duma. The general informed Rodzianko of the Emperor's decision to appoint a new cabinet responsible to the Duma and to entrust its formation to him. Rodzianko replied that evidently neither the Emperor nor the generals realized what was happening, that one of the most terrible revolutions was developing and that he himself, as president of the Duma, was far from being able to contain the rage of the people. The Empress was the object of increasing hatred. A change of ministers and the introduction of ministerial responsibility would have been acceptable on March 12, but now the position of the sovereign himself had become untenable. On all sides rose the demand for the abdication of the Emperor Nicholas in favor of his son Alexei, with a regency of the Grand Duke Mikhail, brother of the Emperor. Rodzianko added that it had been necessary to announce a recall of the troops sent from the front to Petrograd. They had, moreover, been stopped on the way by the revolutionaries.

My friend General Iurii Danilov immediately transmitted a résumé of this conversation from Pskov to Alexeev. General Danilov's communication very clearly confirmed my feeling that there was not one minute to be lost. It was more and more obvious that solutions acceptable one day became impossible the next. On the morning of March 15, I suggested to General Alexeev that he summon the president of the Duma immediately for a direct-line conversation with the purpose of reaching a mutual understanding concerning ways to end the progress of the revolutionary movement. The decisions made would be submitted at once to the chiefs of the armies for their approval, and then, in the name of the Duma and the Army, presented to the Emperor for his acceptance. The general did not wish to accelerate events, and he did not sign the draft of a telegram to Rodzianko written by me to this effect. On the contrary, he asked me to prepare for him a short legal brief on the problems that would arise with a possible abdication of Emperor Nicholas.

I consulted the lawbooks to refresh my memory and immediately drew up the brief the general had requested. I explained that the Fundamental Laws of the Empire did not foresee the abandonment of power by a reigning monarch; however these laws did authorize members of the imperial family so desiring to renounce their rights of succession in expectation of a situation whereby they might be called upon to ascend the throne. There was no reason to refuse that right of renunciation to a member of the reigning family already invested with power.* As for the succession to the throne, it was regulated in the strictest manner by the Fundamental Laws. They stipulated that if the reigning monarch had a son or several sons, it would be this son or the eldest of these sons, minor or not, who should necessarily succeed him on the throne. This order of succession could not be modified by Emperor Nicholas.

In fact, like his predecessors, Nicholas had at the time of his accession solemnly pledged to respect the manner of succession established by the Fundamental Laws. Only an amendment of these laws could introduce a change in the order of succession to the throne. Furthermore, since the reforms of 1906, no change could be made in the Fundamental Laws without the approval of the legislative chambers, that is, the State Council and the Duma. But no Fundamental Law had been enacted to modify the provisions relative to the order of succession. Thus Nicholas II could legally abdicate only in favor of his legitimate heir, his young son Alexei. Since the latter was then only twelve and a half years old, a regency would be required until he reached majority. As for the person of the regent, the Fundamental Laws left Emperor Nicholas free to

* Professor Korkunov, the great specialist in Russian public law, whose courses I took, had supplied such an interpretation of the Fundamental Laws.

choose whomever he wished. When I handed this memorandum to General Alexeev, he said to me: "Your conclusions
confirm what I had thought."

In spite of the extreme gravity of the situation, Alexeev
kept his usual calm and equilibrium, but for anyone who knew
him well it was easy to see that the worthy general felt to the
highest degree the burden of responsibility that weighed upon
him. How often had he warned the Emperor against the disastrous consequences of his erroneous decisions. The obstinacy
of the monarch in persevering on the way to disaster had often
filled his heart with despair. As a faithful soldier, however, he
had never failed in his loyalty to his sovereign and supreme
commander. Except for a few very intimate associates, no one
could know his discontent and his bitterness. It was also extremely painful for him to have to prevail on the Emperor to
renounce the crown. It cost him even more because he had a
clear foreboding of the perturbation that any disturbance of
the imperial power would cause in the country, and he wished
with all his heart to avoid such commotion in a time of war.
Nevertheless, Alexeev realized immediately that no other
solution remained but the abdication of Nicholas II, and he
supported it with the full weight of his authority. To oppose it
would have been to add civil war to the external war.

The fears that a change of monarch inspired were somewhat attenuated by the fact that the abdication of Nicholas II
in favor of his son Alexei would bring about a number of
favorable conditions. This solution would safeguard the legit-
imacy. Because a minor could not renounce his rights, it
would create a situation that could not be legally modified—
at least not for several years. There was a great chance that
the people and the Army would accept the elevation to the
throne of a charming child against whom no grievances could
exist and whose illness would naturally draw sympathy. All
this permitted the hope of maintaining the monarchy and
thereby lessened the risks of a leap into the unknown.

Once his decision was taken, the first concern of General

Alexeev was to ensure the solidarity of the military commanders and to avoid all peril of disunity in the armed forces.
Toward eleven o'clock in the morning he sent identical messages to the commanders of the Army groups, Generals Evert,
Brusilov, and Sakharov, and to the Grand Duke Nicholas
Nikolaevich, commander in chief on the Caucasian front.
General Ruzskii was not consulted because his favorable attitude toward the abdication was already known from the
communications exchanged with him. In his telegram Alexeev
stated that the functioning of the railways and the provisions
for the Army were in fact already in the hands of the new
powers set up in Petrograd. To preserve the Army and prevent
its being contaminated by the internal struggle, the general
saw in the existing situation no other solution than the abdication of Nicholas II. If the military commanders shared his
views, Alexeev urged them to submit their recommendations in
this sense to the Emperor, without delay. All of them replied
immediately, entreating the sovereign to renounce the throne.
At half past two in the afternoon their telegrams were transmitted to Pskov to be presented to Nicholas II together with a
message from Alexeev. The general's message appealed to the
ardent patriotism of Nicholas II and implored him to "make
the decision that God would inspire in him" for the salvation
of Russia.*

The Emperor answered Alexeev immediately that he would
make any sacrifice for the welfare of the country. At the same
time we learned that the Committee of the Duma had sent the
elective member of the State Council, Alexander Guchkov,
and the conservative Duma deputy Vasilii Shulgin to Pskov
to confer with the Emperor, and that they were expected to
arrive there that evening.

---

* The commander of the Baltic fleet, Admiral Nepenin, insisted on the
abdication that evening, without which, in his opinion, the country
would experience the greatest troubles. On March 16 a violent revolt
broke out among the sailors of the Baltic fleet, and the next day Admiral Nepenin was murdered by them.

Alexeev then asked me to draw up the act of abdication. "Put all your heart into it," he added. I shut myself up in my office, and one hour later I returned with the following text: *

In the days of great struggle with an external foe who has been striving for almost three years to enslave our native land, it has been God's will to visit upon Russia a new grievous trial. The internal disturbances which have begun among the people threaten to have a calamitous effect on the future conduct of a hard-fought war. The destiny of Russia, the honor of our heroic Army, the welfare of the people, the whole future of our beloved fatherland demand that the war be carried to a victorious conclusion no matter what the cost. The cruel foe is straining his last resources and the time is already close at hand when our valiant Army, together with our glorious allies, will be able to crush the foe completely. In these decisive days in the life of Russia, We have deemed it Our duty in conscience to help Our people to draw closer together and to unite all the forces of the nation for a speedier attainment of victory, and, in agreement with the State Duma, We have judged it right to abdicate the Throne of the Russian State and to lay down the Supreme Power. In conformance with the order established by the Fundamental Laws, We hand over Our succession to Our beloved Son, the Tsar Successor Tsarevich and Grand Duke Alexei Nikolaevich, and bless Him on his accession to the Throne of the Russian State. We entrust to Our brother, the Grand Duke Mikhail Alexandrovich, the duty of Regent of the Empire until the coming of age of Our Son. We enjoin Our Son, and also until His coming of age the Regent of the Empire, to conduct the affairs of the state in complete and inviolable union with the representatives of the people in the legislative bodies on the principles to be established by them. In the name of the dearly beloved native land, We call upon all true sons of the Fatherland to fulfill their sacred duty to it by their obedience to the Tsar at this hour of national trial and to help Him, together with the people's representatives, to lead

* For a facsimile of the last draft of this text see pages 123 and 124.

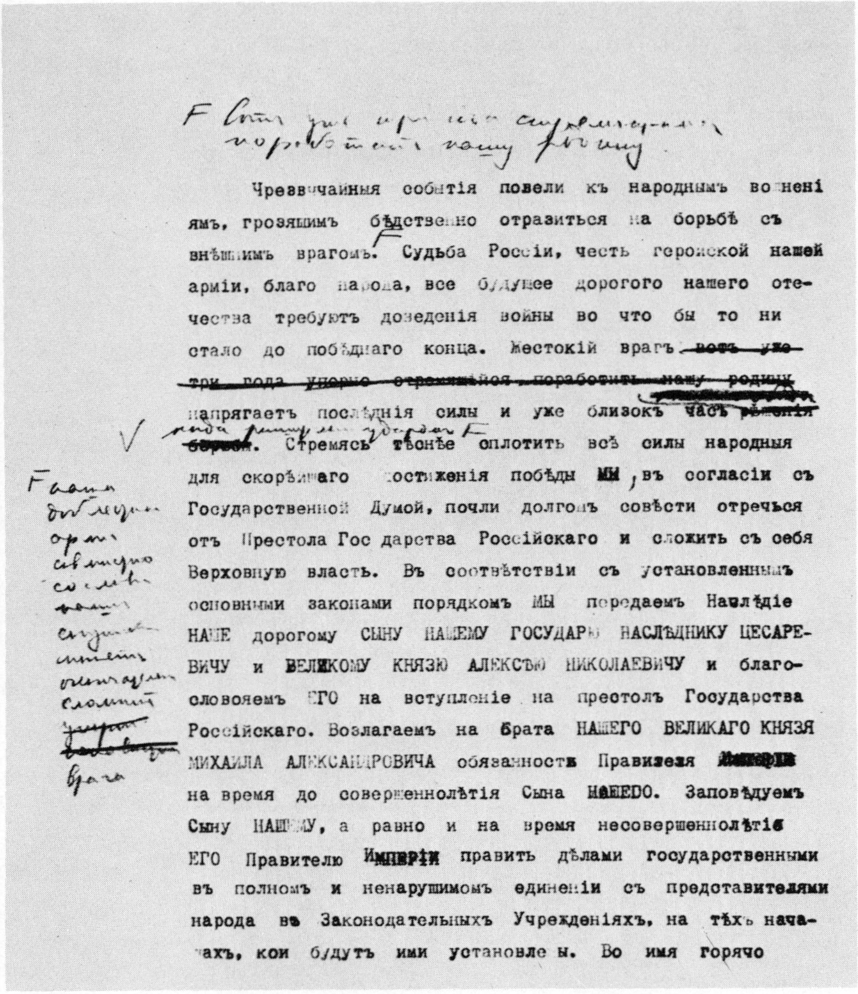

F [handwritten text, illegible] пораборать нашу родину.

Чрезвычайныя событія повели къ народнымъ во ненiямъ, грозящимъ бѣдственно отразиться на борьбѣ съ внѣшнимъ врагомъ. Судьба Россіи, честь геройской нашей арміи, благо народа, все будущее дорогого нашего отечества требуютъ доведенія войны во что бы то ни стало до побѣднаго конца. Жестокій врагъ ~~вотъ уже три года упорно стремившійся поработить нашу родину~~ напрягаетъ послѣднія силы и уже близокъ ~~часъ рѣшенія~~ ~~[handwritten]~~ ~~борьбы~~. Стремясь тѣснѣе сплотить всѣ силы народныя для скорѣйшаго достиженія побѣды МЫ, въ согласіи съ Государственной Думой, почли долгомъ совѣсти отречься отъ Престола Государства Россійскаго и сложить съ себя Верховную власть. Въ соотвѣтствіи съ установленнымъ основными законами порядкомъ МЫ передаемъ Наслѣдіе НАШЕ дорогому СЫНУ НАШЕМУ ГОСУДАРЮ НАСЛѢДНИКУ ЦЕСАРЕВИЧУ и ВЕЛИКОМУ КНЯЗЮ АЛЕКСѢЮ НИКОЛАЕВИЧУ и благословляемъ ЕГО на вступленіе на престолъ Государства Россійскаго. Возлагаемъ на брата НАШЕГО ВЕЛИКАГО КНЯЗЯ МИХАИЛА АЛЕКСАНДРОВИЧА обязанность Правителя ~~Имперіи~~ на время до совершеннолѣтія Сына НАШЕГО. Заповѣдуемъ Сыну НАШЕМУ, а равно и на время несовершеннолѣтія ЕГО Правителю ~~Имперіи~~ править дѣлами государственными въ полномъ и ненарушимомъ единеніи съ представителями народа въ Законодательныхъ Учрежденіяхъ, на тѣхъ началахъ, кои будутъ ими установлены. Во имя горячо

Abdication statement: Basily's draft no. 5

л бимой родины прив ваемъ всѣхъ вѣрныхъ сыновъ Отечества къ ис олненію своего святого долга передъ
ней повиновеніемъ кному ЦАРЮ въ тяжелую годину всенародныхъ испытаній и помочь ЕМУ вмѣстѣ съ представителями народа вывести Россію~~~~~~~~~~~~~~~~~~ на путь
побѣды, благоденствія и славы. Да поможетъ Господь Богъ
Россіи.

Basily wrote on the back of draft No. 4:

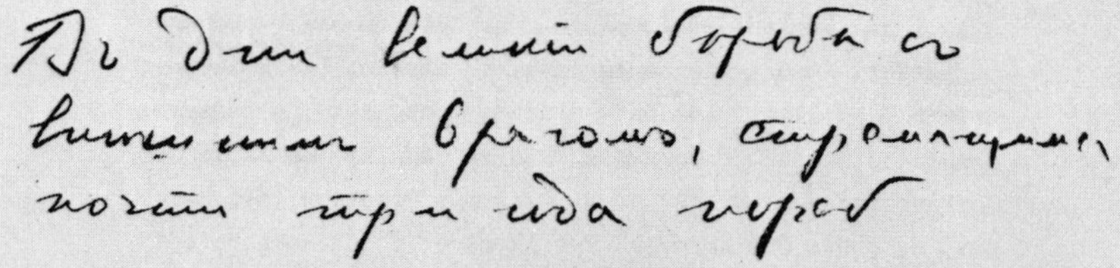

[handwritten text]

General Alekseev accepted this and on back of page 2 of
draft No. 5 changed the opening sentence as follows:

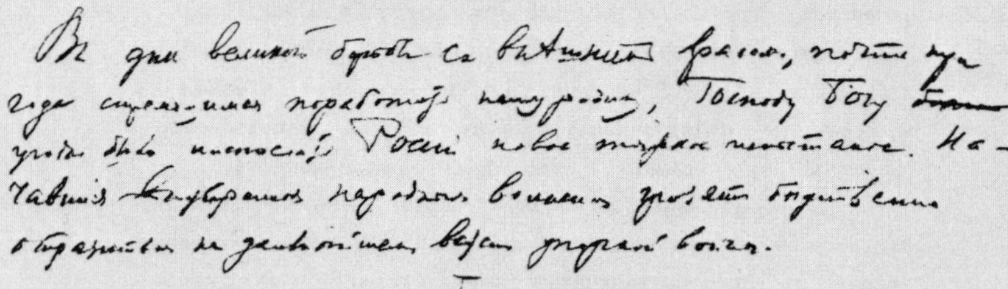

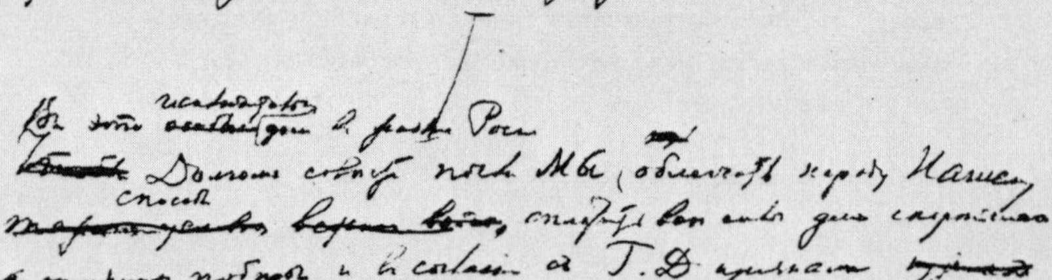

[handwritten text]

the Russian State onto the path of victory, prosperity, and glory. May the Lord God help Russia!

This text was approved without change by General Alexeev, as well as by General Lukomskii and the Grand Duke Sergei Mikhailovich, cousin of the Emperor. I then took it to the chief telegraph operator for Pskov, where it was transmitted that evening toward half past seven.

I spent the evening awaiting the Emperor's reply with the Grand Duke Sergei and a few officers. We had gathered together in the room of the officer on duty, just below Alexeev's office and next to the room housing the Hughes telegraphic apparatus belonging to the General Staff. The little group was nervous, smoking a great deal and exchanging impressions of the situation. The Grand Duke and some of the rest of us were seated on a green rep-covered sofa which together with a few chairs and a large mirror constituted the furnishings of the small room. From time to time General Lukomskii looked in to see if there was any news. Toward half past one in the morning—it was the night of March 15–16—we were advised that a communication would be transmitted from Pskov. We rushed to the telegraph. My eyes never left the ribbon of paper covered with Russian print emerging from the machine. I immediately recognized my text of the abdication manifesto. At first I saw no change, then suddenly I was stupefied to see that the name of the Emperor's son, the young Alexei, had been replaced by that of the Grand Duke Mikhail, brother of Nicholas II. All mention of the regency was omitted. The rest of the manifesto had undergone no change, except that at the end of the second paragraph of my text, after the words, "on the bases established by them" (that is, by the legislative assemblies), the following words had been added in Pskov: "and to swear an inviolable oath to that effect in the name of the beloved country." In the case of little Prince Alexei there would have been no reason for that addition, as a minor cannot take an oath. (For English and Russian texts see Appendix II, p. 187.)

The abdication of Nicholas II in favor of his brother instead of his son was for us a crushing blow indeed. The Grand Duke collapsed on the green sofa, exclaiming: "This is the end!" Those words seemed to answer the question which at that moment filled us all with anguish: Could Mikhail Alexandrovich face the situation and maintain his place on the throne, or would this be the fall of the monarchy? Legally, the Grand Duke Mikhail's claim to the crown was not beyond dispute. Very modest, a man of a gentle nature who preferred to remain in the shadows, he had acquired no personal prestige and was not known to the people. General Alexeev was overwhelmed. If Nicholas II had not left the Stavka, Alexeev would have had an opportunity to defend and perhaps to bring about the only solution that to him seemed practicable—the accession of the legitimate heir, the young Alexei. Why had this solution been set aside? We all asked ourselves this question—without comprehending.

It was not until the following day, when I spoke with the Emperor, that I had the key to the enigma. But for the moment I could not turn my thoughts from the terrible drama Nicholas II had lived through in Pskov, alone, far from his family. I thought of the humiliation, the suffering he must have endured in signing his total failure before the man he considered his greatest enemy—Alexander Guchkov. We knew how the Empress had turned her husband against Guchkov after the latter had unhesitatingly attacked what he considered to be an abuse of the imperial prerogatives. Since then Alexandra, wounded by Guchkov's criticisms, had never acknowledged his firm attachment to the monarchy, his profound patriotism, and his absolute integrity.

Several years later A. Guchkov gave me a signed statement containing his recollections concerning this mission to Nicholas II in Pskov.* Here is the text of that account:

* I did not know Guchkov personally before the March Revolution, but later we became friends.

Vasilii Shulgin and I left for Pskov with a draft manifesto drawn up by Shulgin. We did not intend to insist on this text, but brought it with us only as a suggestion which might aid in the definitive writing of the historic document that was to be composed. At three in the afternoon on March 15 we left the Warsaw station (in Petrograd). The high officials of the railroad gave us every assistance. The train was made up promptly and the order given to proceed at all possible speed.

Our train was held up for quite a while at Gatchina . . . then at Luga, where an enormous crowd of soldiers and bystanders begged me to tell them something, to inform them about the situation.

Toward ten in the evening we arrived at Pskov. General Ruzskii had been advised of our arrival and we planned to talk first with him. We were counting on him to inform us of the Emperor's attitude and thus prepare us for our meeting with him. As soon as the train stopped, however, one of the Emperor's aides-de-camp entered our car and told us, "His Majesty awaits you." It was but a few steps to the imperial train.

We entered a salon car, well lighted and hung with green curtains, where we found Count Fredericks, minister of the Court, and another general, Naryshkin. The Emperor joined us several minutes later. He wore the uniform of one of his Caucasian regiments. His face was calm. As always, his eyes were clear, his gestures serene and measured. No trace of agitation. He greeted us amicably and shook our hands. Then he seated himself in front of a small table. He pointed out my seat, next to him, and Shulgin's, across from him. Count Fredericks took a seat a little farther away. In a corner of the salon General Naryshkin sat at another small table, ready to write. At that moment General Ruzskii entered and, after apologizing to the Emperor, took a seat next to Shulgin, across from the Emperor. Grouped like that—the Emperor, Shulgin, Ruzskii, Fredericks, and myself—we began the conversation.

I spoke first, explaining the situation. In the conditions that had developed, the first thing to do was obviously to repress the uprising. But there were no reliable troops avail-

able; any units of soldiers sent to Petrograd would inevitably
disband as soon as they encountered the incredible de-
moralization that reigned there. General Ruzskii interrupted
to confirm my opinions categorically. I continued, and with
quite genuine emotion I began to speak of the necessity of
abdication. I did not speak at all of the past, but only described the actual state of things, stressing that an abyss was
opening before us. I explained that the only solution would
be the abdication of the Emperor in favor of the heir to the
throne, Alexei, with the designation of the Grand Duke Mikhail Alexandrovich as regent. In conclusion, I mentioned that
the Emperor might wish to collect his thoughts and hear further opinions before making a definitive decision, but that we
would have to resolve the question before our departure,
since the conflagration was spreading rapidly.

The Emperor answered calmly, as if it were a matter of
everyday importance, "I do not have to think any further.
My choice is made. Yesterday and today I weighed everything, and I have decided to renounce the throne. Until three
in the afternoon (of March 15) I was leaning toward abdication in favor of my son, but then I realized that I could not
separate myself from him." At this point he hesitated slightly,
then, with the same self-mastery, he added, "I hope you will
understand me." Finally he said, "Therefore I have decided
to abdicate in favor of my brother." The Tsar got up as if to
leave.

I was speechless. The decision of the Emperor had caught
us unprepared. I had been sure he would abdicate in favor of
his son. A beautiful myth could have been created around
this innocent and pure child. His charm would have helped to
calm the anger of the masses. There could be no controversy
surrounding abdication in favor of a child.

Shulgin then began to speak, expressing the same ideas and
stating that we had considered only the possibility of an abdication in favor of the heir Alexei. I added that we did not
feel it proper to intervene in a matter that related to the feelings of a father and that it was not our role to attempt to
influence him in this regard. My last words brought to the
face of the Emperor an expression of evident satisfaction.

Shulgin supported what I had just said. Finally we expressed our approval of abdication in favor of the Grand Duke Mikhail Alexandrovich.

The Emperor asked us if we could promise that the abdication would truly pacify the country and would not provoke complications. We answered that as far as we could see there would be no difficulties.

V. Shulgin gave the Emperor our draft of the act of abdication in the hope that it might serve as an aid in the elaboration of the final text. The sovereign took our text and went into the next car.

About twenty minutes later, at about 11:15, the Emperor returned to the salon car. He held in his hand an average-sized sheet of paper. He told us, "Here is the act of abdication. Read it." We read it aloud in hushed tones.

The document was well composed, nobly phrased, infinitely better than our draft. I later learned that the text adopted had been sent from the Stavka by telegraph and had been drawn up by Basily.

V. Shulgin asked if it would be possible to insert an addition. To the phrase, "We beg our brother to govern in full and unshakeable concord with the representatives of the nation united in the legislative assemblies, and on the bases established by them," Shulgin proposed to add the words, "and to swear an oath to that effect before the nation." The Tsar expressed agreement immediately and made the minor change, adding this insertion: "and to swear an inviolable oath to that effect."

The act was typed on two or three small sheets of paper. The first page began with the word "Stavka" on the left, and on the right "To the Chief of the General Staff." The signature was in pencil.*

After the drawing up of the act of abdication, I made two requests of the Emperor. I first urged the nomination of Prince Georgii Lvov as president of the Council of Ministers. The Emperor expressed his agreement and added, "I know

---

* The translation of the final text of the abdication document appears as Appendix II of this volume. (Editor's note.)

him." He then asked, "What is his rank?" I answered that I did not know, and Nicholas II smiled.* I next spoke of the necessity for naming a new commander in chief for the Army, and I suggested the Grand Duke Nicholas Nikolae-vich. The Emperor gave his consent immediately.**

It was 11:40 on the night of March 15.***

Because of the uncertainties of the moment, and to save this document from the risk of being destroyed or stolen, I suggested that it be written and signed in two copies. The Emperor agreed.

We left each other with a handshake. The Emperor did not for an instant lose his composure and was at all times friendly with us.

The first copy of the abdication act was to be given to General Ruzskii. The second copy, which was also typed, was on a single large sheet. The Emperor's signature on this copy was likewise in pencil, and was attested at the left by the signature of the minister of the Court, Fredericks. In General Ruzskii's car the copy was given to us to be carried to Petrograd. Shulgin and I acknowledged receipt of the document in writing.

* Under the old regime every civil servant had a rank, which had to be stated in any document relating to nominations. Both Lvov and Guchkov had risen from autonomous local institutions and had not acquired ranking in the civil service. It was unusual for a man to become president of the Council without having earned his stripes in the administration. That is what made Nicholas II smile.
** These two nominations, which were intended to assure continuity in the exercise of power, were immediately placed among the orders signed by the Emperor and dated before the hour of abdication.
*** Guchkov neglects to mention that the act of abdication was dated March 15, 3:00 p.m. (or more exactly March 2, according to the Russian style in use at that time). That was the time at which Nicholas II, having conclusively decided to put down his crown, had signed a first act of abdication, which was in favor of his son. This document he had handed to General Ruzskii. When he later decided to transmit the crown to his brother, he asked Ruzskii to return the first signed text, which he apparently destroyed. In the new act "March 15, 3:00 p.m." was retained to indicate clearly that the abdication had been freely consented to by the sovereign, so that no one could assert that it had been imposed on him by the emissaries of the Committee of the Duma.

We remained in General Ruzskii's car while we waited for a locomotive to be prepared for our return trip. Since we had not eaten, Ruzskii offered us a light meal. General Savich, chief of supplies for the Northern Army Group, joined us. I was distressed by the excessive satisfaction displayed by the two generals: while Shulgin and I were beset by a thousand worries, they were overflowing with joy.

No matter what can be said of me, no matter what charges can be imputed to me, I state clearly that I had never been the enemy of the Emperor. Yes, I considered him incapable of exercising power. Even in normal times he was not equal to his task; he was even less prepared for the tragic times this immense empire was now passing through. In that historic moment, however, I felt only an immense pity for him. I thought, "My God, why was it his fate to carry the weight of such a heavy crown?" And in my heart grew an intense anger against all the worthless beings who had surrounded this unfortunate Emperor.*

(signed) A. Guchkov**

Even as Guchkov and Shulgin set out on their trip to Petrograd, the imperial train departed from Pskov, towards three o'clock in the morning, on the way to Mogilev, the former

* General Cyril Naryshkin told me that Guchkov and Shulgin appeared devastated by these events and behaved in the most respectful manner vis-à-vis the Emperor. While he was explaining the situation to the Emperor, Guchkov kept his face turned down, his eyes fixed on the table before him, his brow supported by one hand. (That was one of his familiar poses, one which I often noticed later when he was making an effort to concentrate.) The Emperor, imperturbable and dignified, gazed straight ahead.

** The intimate journal of Nicholas II, published by the Bolsheviks after his assassination, revealed the bitterness which he felt during these tragic hours and which he hid behind the mask of his habitual impassiveness. On March 15, the same day as his abdication, he made the following entry: "Around me there is nothing but treason, cowardice, and deception." It is true that Emperor Nicholas met with much disaffection during the last years of his reign, but it is equally certain that many of those who had hoped he would listen to wise counsels remained completely loyal to him and sought only to ward off the catastrophe.

monarch having expressed a desire to bid goodbye to his collaborators and to the Army. By the time Nicholas II and the emissaries of the Duma arrived at their respective destinations, the situation was to have changed greatly.

But let us return to our observation post, the General Headquarters, or Stavka. General Alexeev had scarcely had time to recover from the shock of the abdication of Nicholas II in favor of his brother when, on March 16 at six o'clock in the morning, he was called to the Hughes apparatus by Rodzianko, who had asked to confer with him. The president of the Duma first requested that the general stop publication to the Army of the manifesto signed by Nicholas II.* Rodzianko explained that the accession of the young Alexei under the regency of the Grand Duke Mikhail would probably have been accepted, but that the elevation to the throne of the latter would meet with insurmountable opposition.

As a matter of fact, on the afternoon of March 15, resentment against the fallen regime had provoked a frightful revolt among the undisciplined soldiers of the Petrograd garrison, with cries of "Down with the Romanovs!" "Down with the officers!" "Land and liberty!" ** Many officers had been massacred. Crowds of workmen had joined the soldiers. Under these conditions, to announce the accession of the Grand Duke Mikhail to the throne would only add fuel to the fire of revolt. These passions had subsided only after laborious negotiations during the night, when the Committee of the Duma was able to come to a mutual understanding with the leaders of the Soviet. A Constituent Assembly, to be elected by direct and universal suffrage, would be convoked at the earliest possible time. That assembly would decide the future form of government in Russia. In the meantime the country would be

* During the same morning Rodzianko repeated to General Ruzskii in greater detail what he had just told Alexeev. The text of Rodzianko's communication to Ruzskii was immediately sent to the Stavka.
** This "Land and liberty" demand was the favorite slogan of the Socialist-Revolutionary Party, determined adversaries of the dynasty and advocates of the distribution of all land to the peasants.

ruled by a Provisional Government formed by the Duma Committee. Having no forces to support them in subduing the insurgents, the moderate elements of the Duma found no other solution but a compromise with the Soviet. This was the sole means of retaining any power in their own hands and keeping the door open for an eventual reestablishment of the monarchy. Rodzianko concluded on an optimistic note. He expressed the conviction that the solution they had adopted would provoke a powerful wave of patriotic enthusiasm and would assure tranquility to the country and lead to victory.

Could Rodzianko sincerely have entertained such illusions? Was he not rather trying to persuade himself? In any case, he had no other course to pursue than the one outlined by him. It was not possible to continue the war and at the same time suppress the riots in Petrograd. And what troops would lend themselves to crushing the insurgents?

Rodzianko's message made it quite evident that the masses were falling more and more under the influence of those who, according to an expression then current in Russia, were seeking to "develop the revolution in depth." The insurrection in Petrograd had been a surprise not only for the moderate groups but also for the parties of the extreme left. It could hardly have been the work of the latter inasmuch as their clandestine organizations had been largely destroyed by the police since 1914. The socialists, however, were not long in resuming the offensive and exploiting the opportunity offered to them. The imperial regime had delayed in making the possession of land more accessible and a still too-small percentage of the population could enjoy the advantages of owning property. It was this which accounted for the success of the socialists with the masses. Now that the prestige of the monarchy had been so strongly shaken, they became easier prey than before for propaganda in favor of a socialist republic. Also, the extremist parties hastened to intensify their activities in the rural districts and above all among the troops. If they succeeded, the upheaval obviously would be total and the country would have to bear grave consequences. Would the Provisional Government mentioned by Rodzianko have the necessary authority to check the revolutionary movement, to maintain order and direct the transition to a new political and social organization of the vast nation? What men would be called for that heavy task?

The telegraph had just announced to us the definitive list of members of this Provisional Government, indicating the portfolio assigned to each. Here is the composition of this new government:

President of the Council and Minister of the Interior	Prince G. Lvov
Minister of Foreign Affairs	P. Miliukov
Minister of Justice	A. Kerenskii
Minister of Transport	N. Nekrasov
Minister of Commerce	A. Konovalov
Minister of Public Instruction	A. Manuilov
Minister of War and the Navy	A. Guchkov
Minister of Agriculture	A. Shingarev
Minister of Finance	M. Tereshchenko
Controller of State Accounts	I. Godnev
Procuror of the Holy Synod	Vladimir Lvov

The eminent, wise, and experienced civil servants open to the ideas of our age had been, one by one, eliminated by action of the Empress, and replaced, through her influence, either by insignificant functionaries or by valets of reaction. Now, after the revolution which had just taken place, the administration of the country would find itself in the hands of political men. Certainly they were men of good intentions and incontestable patriotism, but until now they had been dedicated first of all to the opposition and hence lacked experience in the exercise of power, a circumstance particularly grave in view of the critical conditions the country was now going through. Except for Kerenskii, the new ministers all professed liberal and moderate ideas and belonged to circles that were "bourgeois," in the language of the socialists. Kerenskii, a member of the Socialist-Revolutionary Party, was the only link between the Provisional Government and the socialist parties which dominated the Petrograd Soviet. Obviously the moderate orientation of the members of the Provisional Government was comforting for us at Headquarters, but we asked ourselves with the greatest anxiety how they would be able to resist the socialist demands, which were steadily becoming louder and louder.

Toward three o'clock in the afternoon (still March 16), General Alexeev had me called and requested that I go to meet the imperial train and inform the Emperor of the latest events. A locomotive and a railway car were immediately prepared, and at half past three I left the Mogilev station. I carried with me a small notebook bound in black leather, in which I had made a résumé, day by day, of the principal communications received at the Stavka, or sent by the Stavka, since the outbreak of the revolution. The sun was sinking, and the snow on the fields and the trees of the forests glittered in its light.

At a little before six o'clock we reached Orsha, and the chief of my convoy came to tell me that we would wait there for the imperial train, which had already been announced. I had time to take only a few steps on the deserted platform of that little station when I caught sight of the gold-trimmed blue cars of the imperial train slowly approaching. General Count Grabbe, commander of the Tsar's escort, was at the door of one of the carriages and invited me to enter as soon as the train had stopped. Colonel Anatoli A. Mordvinov, the Emperor's aide-de-camp then on duty, announced me immediately to the sovereign. In his memoirs,* Mordvinov relates that I looked utterly defeated and that, to all evidence, I was

* *Russkaia letopis,* no. 5 (Paris, 1923), p. 132.

horror-stricken at what was happening. My emotion was increased still more by my misgivings about seeing the Emperor again in such painful circumstances.

As soon as I was in the Emperor's presence, his own self-control revived me. Nicholas II received me in a small compartment which served as an office. A mahogany writing table stood under the window, and beside it was a sofa covered with green fabric.

The Emperor came forward amiably to meet me, and I explained to him the reason for my visit. He motioned me to a small desk armchair in front of the table and seated himself on the sofa. He was dressed in the gray plastun uniform of a Caucasian infantry regiment. His face and his small beard were as carefully groomed as ever. His expression was absolutely calm, and betrayed no trace of emotion. The look in his fine blue eyes was affable as always.

Referring to the notes in my small notebook, I summed up for him, as briefly as possible, the news that had reached us during the last few days describing a situation that was becoming more and more desperate. Everything was collapsing. The capital had refused to accept the succession of the Grand Duke Mikhail to the throne. The dynasty was in danger of falling; the country was adrift.

The Emperor listened, impassive. Each time I finished giving him some piece of information, he would say, "But yes, naturally," * in the most quiet voice. I was stupefied by the calm of his replies, by his extraordinary self-possession. I could not believe my eyes, or my ears. This "but yes, naturally," repeated itself like a refrain all during my report, and the restrained sound of his voice repeating those words remains forever engraved in my memory. He manifested no astonishment at the turn that events had taken in so short a time. One would even have thought he expected it. The Emperor's extraordinarily calm attitude permitted me to tell him, at the end of my report, how distressed we were that he had

* In Russian, *"Nu da, konechno."*

not followed General Alexeev's suggestion and abdicated in favor of his son. He replied very simply: "You know that my son is ill. I could not separate myself from him."

At the end of the interview the Emperor rose and shook my hand. Then, after a moment of hesitation, he asked me: "Do you wish to return to Mogilev in your train, or do you prefer to go back with me?" Did the Emperor, with his innate delicacy, already fear to compromise in the eyes of the new power the persons who remained with him? This thought was very painful to me, and I replied to the Emperor that I would be infinitely happy to accompany him. Nicholas II smiled amiably.

I left him filled with admiration for his dignity, for his stoicism in the face of adversity. He had been virtually deposed without anyone's lifting a hand to defend him. He spoke of it as of a thing that did not touch him. He accepted fate without the least revolt, without the least show of anger or ill humor, without the least reproach to anyone. This man, who on so many occasions had seemed to us to lack will, had made his decision with great courage and dignity, without hesitation. Now that his destiny demanded the sacrifice, he accepted it with all his heart, with real grandeur. According to the English expression, he knew how to lose.

After having taken leave of the Emperor, I remembered that I had forgotten to give him any news of his family. I therefore asked to see him again for an instant and told him that, according to the last information received at the Stavka, the Empress and her children were still at Tsarskoe Selo and had not been molested.

I went to join the Emperor's suite, who were waiting for me impatiently. During that memorable journey the Emperor was accompanied by the following ten persons: the old Count Fredericks, minister of the Court; General for the Suite V. Voieikov, the commander of the Palace; Prince Vasilii Dolgorukov, a marshal of the Court; General-Admiral C. Nilov, an aide-de-camp; General for the Suite Cyril Naryshkin; General for the Suite Count A. Grabbe; the Emperor's doctor, Professor S. Fedorov; two service adjutants, Colonel Duke Nicholas of Leuchtenberg and Colonel A. Mordvinov; and the chief of the imperial trains, the engineer Ezhov.

In his memoirs Mordvinov relates that in passing the compartment of General Voieikov, I expressed astonishment that this man could survive after what had just happened. It always seemed to me that he had made himself the Empress's instrument in the Emperor's entourage, and that of all the Tsar's intimates he was the element most opposed to influences that were not even liberal but simply reasonable. My memory evoked the occasions when, by malevolent and gratuitous insinuation, Voieikov had sought to turn me away from my attachment to those loyal servants of the crown who had had the merit to warn the Emperor of the dangers of his reactionary policy, and the times when I had been obliged to express to this general my admiration for these real patriots. Did Voieikov now feel the weight of his responsibility? In spite of a controlled demeanor he seemed to be greatly affected and quite stupefied by the catastrophe.

Grabbe asked me into his compartment, where the others joined us. Briefly, I informed them of the latest events. Good old Count Fredericks was completely dismayed; Naryshkin was quiet. Dolgorukov, a man of great nobility of character, kept his composure as did the excellent Duke of Leuchtenberg, who did not belong to the regular suite. Later I spoke for a few minutes with Professor Fedorov. He told me that the day before, when the Emperor had made his decision to abdicate, Nicholas II called for him and asked him if the young Grand Duke Alexei would really never be well. Fedorov replied that there was, at least for the moment, no indication permitting the hope that hemophilia could be cured. It was after having listened to this opinion concerning the hopeless malady of his son that Nicholas II concluded it would be impossible to be separated from him and made the decision to renounce the throne in favor of his brother.

Dinner was announced. The guests assembled in the salon preceding the dining room, where hors d'oeuvre were served. The Emperor joined us. He remained silent, and conversation began only when we followed the Emperor into the dining room. The Emperor seated himself, and Count Fredericks, minister of the Court, sat down opposite him. On the Emperor's right were Nilov, Grabbe, and Dolgorukov; on the sovereign's left were Voieikov and Naryshkin. On the right of Count Fredericks, Fedorov and Mordvinov took their places, and on the left of the minister of the Court, Ezhov and the Duke of Leuchtenberg, beside whom—and facing Dolgorukov —a place had been added for me. Seated on the side opposite Nicholas II, I could observe him very well.

At first the Emperor was taciturn. Although his face remained always impassive, violent contractions shook the muscles of his throat from time to time, betraying the moral suffering that he otherwise succeeded so well in hiding. Anyone occupying my place at this dinner could never believe in the so-called insensibility that had been attributed to Nicholas II because of his extraordinary self-mastery. I spoke with my neighbor and my vis-à-vis, who questioned me constantly. They asked the composition of the Provisional Government, and I showed them the list of the new ministers. The Emperor paid attention to our discourse, and we passed to him my little black notebook in which he read the names of the members of the Provisional Government.* He questioned me about them, particularly those he had not met or about whom he desired to be better informed.

After dinner the Emperor retired and the rest of us returned to the salon next to the dining room. Naryshkin explained to me then that the Emperor's interview with Guchkov and Shulgin had taken place in this same salon the night before. He pointed out a small table standing before a window where

* This notebook still remains in my possession. (This notebook is now part of the Nicolas de Basily Papers in the Archives of the Hoover Institution. Editor's note.)

Nicholas II had sat with the emissaries of the Duma, and described to me the historic scene he had witnessed in this compartment. His account coincided in all particulars with what Guchkov later set down for me in the statement reproduced above.

The imperial train reached Mogilev at twenty minutes past eight in the evening. The personnel of the Stavka with General Alexeev at their head, as well as the Grand Dukes Sergei Mikhailovich and Boris Vladimirovich, were assembled at the railway station to meet the Emperor. I immediately took my place among the chiefs of services of the General Headquarters.

Nicholas II approached General Alexeev and embraced him, then he slowly walked among the persons present. In silence he saluted each one of us with a handshake, looking into our eyes. All were greatly moved, and stifled sobs could be heard. The Emperor kept his apparent calm. From time to time he threw back his head in a movement customary to him. A few tears formed in the corners of his eyes and he brushed them away with a gesture of his hand.

The emotions that shook the witnesses of this scene derived from a throng of sentiments. We had so often deplored the poor judgment of Nicholas II, so many times we had criticized his blindness, and yet we could not judge him too harshly for his errors knowing that the responsibility for his unfortunate decisions rested primarily with the Empress Alexandra. We pitied the Emperor's weakness in the face of his wife, the unconscious factor of his failure. Was not Nicholas II, in the manner of the heroes of the Greek tragedies, the predestined victim of an implacable fate? It was preordained that the woman he married—a German princess, granddaughter of Queen Victoria of England—should embrace the cause of Russian autocracy with such fervor that she inspired in her husband a firm will to resist any attack on the imperial prerogatives. Fate also decreed that a kind of monk, the false and debauched Grigorii Rasputin, who in some mysterious manner twice arrested near-fatal hemophilia crises for the Grand Duke Alexei, should appear in the eyes of the anguished, mystical Empress as a "man of God" and thereby acquire such influence in the affairs of state that he became the grave-digger of the tsarist regime. Had not some of us, facing the danger which menaced the monarchy, reproached ourselves at times for having remained loyal to our sovereign when a coup d'état to replace him on the throne by another member of the dynasty might perhaps have averted the catastrophe? In spite of his faults as a sovereign, Nicholas II as a man had never inspired in us anything other than sympathy and even affection. All his life he had sought to do what he considered to be his duty. As a private individual he would have been a model of virtue. And then, for almost twenty-five years he had been the symbol of our country, as his ancestors, the builders of the Russian Empire, had been. Without the Tsar what would Russia become? We had served Nicholas II to the best of our ability, and yet not one of us, and no one in Russia, had attempted to defend his crown. It was obvious that all intervention in this sense would have been not only useless but disastrous. All these thoughts came to our minds as we bowed before our Emperor, a man fallen yet grown in stature through the moral courage he gave proof of in adversity.

The last sojourn of Nicholas II in Mogilev lasted five days. There he prepared his farewell order to the armies, a message written by him in terms of the most fervent patriotism and in complete forgetfulness of self. In expressing his wishes for the success of the Provisional Government and inviting everyone to serve it, he terminated his reign with a declaration of great nobility. This is the text of that farewell order:

> For the last time I address you, armies so dear to my heart! Since I have, in my name and in that of my son, renounced the throne of Russia, the power has been transmitted to the Provisional Government which has been formed at the initiative of the Duma of the Empire.

May God help this Government to lead Russia toward glory and prosperity! May God also help you to defend our country against a cruel enemy! During more than two and a half years you have ceaselessly endured the rough hardships of war. Much blood has been shed, great efforts have been accomplished, and already the hour is near when Russia, united with her valiant allies in a common cause, will break the last resistance of the enemy. This unprecedented war must be pursued to a definitive victory.

Whosoever thinks of immediate peace, whosoever desires it, is a traitor to the country. I know that all good soldiers think thus. Therefore, do your duty, defend our great fatherland courageously. Serve the Provisional Government, obey your chiefs, and remember that any relaxation of discipline will only serve the interests of the enemy.

I have the firm conviction that a boundless love for our beautiful fatherland still burns in your hearts. May God bless you, and may Saint George, the great martyr, lead you to victory!

Nicholas.

Stavka, March 21, 1917

The Provisional Government did not think it could permit this message to be officially communicated to the troops; this publication ban on the document was profoundly distressing to many of us. The text became known, however, through private copies which circulated among the troops and the public.

On March 21 Nicholas II was taken to Tsarskoe Selo by some delegates of the Provisional Government who came to arrest him and also to protect him.

As Rodzianko had already foreseen when he had his conversation with Alexeev at dawn on March 16, the abdication of Nicholas II was followed in less than twenty-four hours by the Grand Duke Mikhail's renunciation of the throne. The circumstances under which the brother of the fallen monarch made this decision were related by Alexander Guchkov in the following note, which he dictated for me:

> After the abdication of Nicholas II Shulgin and I returned to Petrograd. At about ten o'clock in the morning on March 16, while I was still at the station, I received an urgent message from Rodzianko. He asked me not to spread the news of the abdication (of Nicholas II) and summoned me immediately to the apartment of the Grand Duke Mikhail Alexandrovich. . . . When I arrived there, I found a meeting already under way. The small and intimate salon of the Grand Duke was filled with people. About fifteen persons were there, notably Rodzianko, Lvov, Miliukov, Godnev, and the others (members of the Provisional Committee of the Duma). The Grand Duke was seated on a sofa. The members of the Duma were grouped around him either sitting or standing. I entered quietly and was utterly stupefied. I listened and could not believe my ears.
>
> With ardor and instistence, Rodzianko was exhorting the Grand Duke Mikhail not to accept the crown. He explained how unfortunate it would be if his accession to the throne were to be marred by bloodshed. Konovalov energetically supported Rodzianko. From all corners there was great pressure on the Grand Duke. Everyone was pointing out the danger of a civil war.* I did not understand a thing. Just the preceding day, before my departure, there had been no question of any such turn of events. What had happened?
>
> I took Godnev to one side and asked him, "For the love of God, will you explain to me what has been going on?" He informed me that the preceding night had been rich in events. The revolutionary conflagration had intensified. The masses

---

* It is necessary to add to Guchkov's account that Kerenskii, in spirited language, was trying to persuade the Grand Duke Mikhail to refuse the throne. He explained that his advice was dictated not by his republican opinions but purely by the interests of the country. The anger of the workers and soldiers, he asserted, was above all directed against the monarchy and any attempt to maintain it would provoke a civil war, which would be made even worse by the external conflict. In concluding, he warned the Grand Duke that if he accepted the crown his life would be in danger.

had been caught up in a frenzy of excitement. All sides had sent delegations. Everyone, including Rodzianko, Lvov, and their colleagues, had come to the conclusion that the accession of the Grand Duke Mikhail to the throne was impossible. Only Miliukov held out, proclaiming that the renunciation of Mikhail was inadmissible.

I asked to speak. I clearly and firmly expressed the opinion that Grand Duke Mikhail must occupy the throne. The nation could not be without a head. If absolutely necessary, I would agree to accept that if the Grand Duke Mikhail were to assume the crown, he would take the obligation to convoke a constituent assembly after the war that would bespeak the national will. At the very least, the Grand Duke must assume the regency.

Miliukov once more energetically pleaded the necessity of the Grand Duke's accession to the throne, but he declared himself opposed to my suggestion relating to a regency. A regency, he said, could not be juridically instituted except upon the death or illness of a monarch. After again requesting the floor to develop my ideas, I renewed my insistence that the Grand Duke accept the throne, and as for the question of a regency, I held that the state of war could justify recourse to that expediency. I was the last to speak.

The Grand Duke then said that he wanted time for reflection and moved toward the door of the salon. Before he left, Kerenskii asked him not to communicate with anyone by telephone. Kerenskii apparently feared that the Grand Duke would consult with his wife, who was considered very ambitious (and who moreover was thought to have been won over to the ideas of the K. D. Party). With a smile, the Grand Duke acquiesced. A few moments later, he returned and asked to speak privately with Rodzianko and Lvov. Then the three walked away to speak among themselves.

I took advantage of the moment to go to the telephone and inform my family that I had returned from Pskov. These were fearful days and I was worried that they might be concerned for my safety. Suddenly I saw Kerenskii next to me. "Where are you telephoning? Whom do you want to talk to?" I answered that I was going to speak with my wife. He left me. I returned to the salon, and the Grand Duke, Rodzianko, and Lvov soon rejoined us.

The Grand Duke stated in a firm voice that he was going to renounce the throne.

Very moved, I said to all who were there, "Gentlemen, I refuse to follow you. You are leading the country to ruin." Kerenskii set about trying to persuade me to remain part of the ministry, at least for the time being, and not to provoke any discord.

The Grand Duke did not sign any papers at this meeting. I recall that Vladimir Nabokov and Baron Nolde * then explained the act that the Grand Duke would have to sign.

(signed) A. Guchkov

The Grand Duke Mikhail's act of abdication was signed early in the afternoon of March 16 and published during the night, at the same time as that of Emperor Nicholas II. The renunciation of the Grand Duke Mikhail to the succession of his brother was formulated in these terms:

A heavy burden has been laid on me by my brother, who has passed over to me the imperial throne of Russia at a time of unprecedented war and popular disturbances.

Animated by the thought which is in the minds of all, that the good of the State is above other considerations, I have decided to accept the supreme power only if that be the desire of our great people, expressed at a general election for their representatives to the Constituent Assembly, which should determine the form of government and lay down the fundamental laws of the Russian Empire.

With a prayer to God for His blessings, I beseech all citizens of the Empire to subject themselves to the Provisional Government, which is created by and invested with full power by the State Duma until the summoning, at the earliest possible moment, of a Constituent Assembly, selected by uni-

* These were two jurisconsults called to the residence of the Grand Duke at the end of the meeting to write his act of abdication.

versal, direct, equal, and secret ballot, which shall establish a government in accordance with the will of the people.

March 16, 1917   Mikhail

A few days later one of the authors of this text, my old friend Baron Boris Nolde, explained to me that the phrase "I beseech all the citizens of the Empire to subject themselves to the Provisional Government, which is created by and invested with full power by the State Duma" was written in order not only to establish the transfer of supreme power to the new government but also to endow that government with the right to issue laws. Obviously this was a weak legal formulàtion, but one had to be content with it, having nothing better. Its purpose of assuring at least a semblance of continuity between the powers of the monarchy and those of the Provisional Government corresponded well with the state of mind of the Provisional Government's members. They did not wish to owe their power to the rebellion, to the street, and were concerned with legality, whereas the Petrograd Soviet boasted of its purely revolutionary origin and in moving toward the triumph of socialism rejected all ties with the past.

In preceding chapters I have had occasion to speak of the principal defects from which Imperial Russia suffered: the peasant's intense desire for the lands still in the possession of the upper classes, and the great distance that separated the masses of the population from the thin layer of cultivated elements, both in manner of living and in mode of thought. These two controversial aspects of Russian life had in a certain measure already been attenuated, but they still remained pronounced enough to compromise the solidity of the regime. So these evils determined the course that the Russian revolution followed in its development. They were not, however, the direct causes of the revolutionary tempest of March 1917 that overthrew the monarchy. That sudden explosion was provoked first of all by economic disorganization brought on by the war and by the incapacity of the government to find a remedy, then by the fatigue of soldiers wearied by an unhappy war, and finally and above all by the fact that the imperial power had lost its prestige.

Ill-chosen ministers, ministerial incompetence, and governmental inattention to the social aspirations of the masses and the political aspirations of the elite, resulted in the disaffection of the whole nation from the established regime. Under these conditions, it had sufficed that a few thousand soldiers should mutiny in the barracks of reserve units in the capital, and a political structure that had lasted for long centuries collapsed in five days.

This was all the greater pity in that—to any informed witness of the last years of the reign of Nicholas II—it was completely evident that a little wisdom in the exercise of power would have enabled the monarchy to avoid the reefs upon which it was wrecked. The patriotic spirit which rallied the whole nation around the throne in the beginning of the war offered a unique opportunity to lead Russia toward a progressive transformation based on a better political and social balance. Alas, the monarch took the opposite course. Had he been better inspired, had he leaned upon the dynamic forces of the nation, he would probably have been able to hold the country together until the end of the war instead of sinking with it in the catastrophe.

A part of the responsibility in the collapse of the imperial regime also falls upon the Russian upper class. The majority of the landed nobility, frightened by the agrarian claims of the peasants in the First Duma, turned resolutely toward reaction and exercised an unfortunate influence in this direction on the government. As for the liberal parties—and in particular the Cadets, who were in despair over the blindness of the Tsar and the Empress—they finished by attacking the imperial power publicly and openly and thus contributed to the definitive ruin of what imperial prestige might still have remained. It was an irony of fate that all these enlightened partisans of the monarchy helped it to commit suicide when they should have made every effort to save it in spite of itself. However, if instead of discrediting the regime in the eyes of the public, they had secretly prepared and realized a timely coup d'état to replace the person of the sovereign by another member of the dynasty, they might perhaps have given the monarchy a last chance to repair its errors and maintain itself, even if only until the end of the war. It is true that there were some vague plans for a conspiracy, but these did not have time to take shape before they were forestalled by the popular insurrection. Those in the thin civilized stratum let themselves be surprised by events because they did not sufficiently recognize their own weakness. They forgot that a profound gulf had always separated them from the ignorant popular masses and they had not yet acquired any grasp of the mass mentality. They also tended to forget that the elite, created by Peter the Great and strengthened by his successors, had not ceased to be bound to the fate of the monarchy, which still remained the only source of authority in the country. If this power should fail, the elite would necessarily find itself at the mercy of the ignorant, hostile masses, and would follow the monarchy to its ruin.

Appendix I

Appendix 1

SECRET

ON OUR GOALS IN REGARD
TO THE STRAITS

MEMORANDUM by
N. A. de BASILY

NOVEMBER 1914

The historic Question of the Straits has economic, strategic, and general political importance for Russia.

I

The waterway through the Straits is for us an essential commercial artery. Its importance for our exports is evident from the following figures.

Year	Exports from Russia through the Dardanelles	Total exports from the Empire
	(Millions of rubles)	
1903	410	1,001
1904	410	1,006
1905	406	1,007
1906	378	1,094
1907	386	1,053
1908	345	998
1909	565	1,427
1910	565	1,449
1911	568	1,591
1912 *	433	1,518

* The drop in exports through the Dardanelles in 1912 was due to the temporary closing of the Straits during the Italian-Turkish war. The above figures are established on the basis of data furnished by the Ministry of Trade and Industry.

On the average, exports through the Dardanelles during that decade amounted to 37 per cent of the total exports of the Empire.

Shipment of our exports through the Straits cannot be replaced by overland transportation. The latter is on the average 25 times more expensive than shipment by sea. Besides, our exports from the Black Sea consist in general of grain and raw materials. This kind of freight cannot tolerate high shipping rates.

The primary importance of the Straits trade route was amply demonstrated in 1912 and 1913, when even their temporary closing by Turkey had a strongly adverse effect on our whole economy.

The losses caused to us then amounted to over 30 million rubles every month. According to a memorandum which the minister of finance attached to the preliminary budget plans for 1914, the trade balance of Russia in 1912 dropped one hundred million rubles below the average active balance for the preceding three years. The cause of this was found to be in unsatisfactory sales of the harvest: in addition to unfavorable weather, grain export obstacles arose because of the temporary closure of the Dardanelles to commercial shipping. As a consequence, the State Bank was compelled in the spring of 1913 to raise the rate of discount for three-month promissory notes by .5 per cent. This is a proof of the strong impact on our economy of any interruption of shipments through the Straits.

It is certain that the importance for Russia of the trade route through the Straits will greatly increase in the future. The economic growth of our Southern provinces goes on very rapidly and successfully. We may expect that our Southern provinces will be transformed into a rich industrial region owing to their abundance of iron ore and coal and their proximity to the Black Sea coast. This is bound to produce increased trade through the Black Sea. The development of railroads and the growing exploitation of natural resources in the economic hinterlands of the Black Sea areas, and in particular in Persia, will have a similar effect on that trade.

The freedom of the commercial waterway out of the Black Sea into the Mediterranean and back is therefore a necessary condition for the normal economic life of Russia and for the further development of her prosperity.*

* That this fact was recognized long ago is evident from the works of the French Publicist [Jean-Louis] Favier, who wrote in 1773: "The

Yet, as the situation stands now, we cannot consider that a free flow of our trade through the Straits is secure. Events of past years have shown that when Turkey has found it to her advantage she has closed the Straits, even for lengthy periods, without taking our interests into consideration. If [Turkey's] mining the Straits at the time of the Italian-Turkish and Greco-Turkish wars was required by defense considerations, the closure of the Straits in the middle of September 1914, when Turkey was not at war with anyone, was nothing but gross abuse.

Our most important trade route depends on the arbitrary rule of an alien territorial Power and its international relations. This creates a situation that is not only contrary to the paramount interests of our country but humiliating to our prestige.

From the point of view of economics, our goal in regard to the Straits should be the establishment of guarantees for the unhindered use of this waterway for our trade.

These guarantees should be practicable. Legal guarantees alone will not suffice in this case. These would be of value only in periods of peace; in case of war their practicability would depend on safeguarding by force. Therefore, without sanctions such guarantees would be worthless.

Such guarantees could be absolutely secure only if the whole waterway through the Straits were somehow to be placed under our authority. Only if the defense of that road is in our hands can we be assured that it will be protected at all times from anyone's encroachments. Less complete guarantees will, of course, offer less security.

But it is necessary to keep in mind that even the establishment of our authority over the Straits would not afford us an absolutely secure economic outlet into the Mediterranean. In the case of a war against us, it would still be possible for a country possessing a sufficiently strong navy in the Mediterranean to proclaim and carry out a blockade of the Straits.

war between Russia and Turkey is first of all a trade war, because for Russia the Black Sea trade has the same importance as the trade with America has for France, Spain, and England."

II

The strategic importance of the Straits resides in the fact that the power which controls them can prevent warships from passing from the Mediterranean into the Black Sea and back, and can do this at its own discretion, without having to use important naval forces. Moreover the Straits provide an excellent operational base for any naval action in the Mediterranean as well as in the Black Sea.

As the Straits consist of two consecutive defiles—the Bosporus and the Dardanelles—the control of both insures the free passage of ships from one sea into the other. The control of but one of them can only prevent the exit of ships into the sea adjacent to that particular defile.

When we speak of the Dardanelles defile, not only the defile itself should be considered but also the expanse of sea lying between it and the adjoining group of Aegean islands: Tenedos, Imbros, Samothrace, and Lemnos. These islands are close enough to the Dardanelles that they can be in varying degrees useful in the prevention of any exit from the Straits.

Modern military technique offers many possibilities for preventing an alien fleet from passing through a defile.

Owing to their narrowness and depth, the Bosporus and the Dardanelles fulfill conditions which would permit them to be closed by the following means:

1) Coastal artillery;
2) Torpedoes fired from tubes on the shores;
3) Obstruction of the waterway by underwater mines;
4) Submarine activity in the Straits.

All these means can be put to use only if one has control over the shores of the Straits. It is evident that such control is necessary to allow the installation of coastal artillery and torpedo tubes. Underwater mines would be efficient only if protected by coastal artillery that could prevent their removal by minesweepers.* Sub-

* If one had no control over the shores of the Straits, their closure by mines would be effective for only a short time before the mines were removed by minesweepers. Such action could be hindered by naval action only if the country controlling the Straits had not established satisfactory defenses beforehand.

marines could be used in the Straits only if they were not exposed
to danger from the shores, as their periscopes could be spotted
and they could then be destroyed by coast artillery.

From the military-naval point of view, foreign domination of
the Straits has for us the following adverse consequences.

The control over the Dardanelles defile (including, as stated
above, the narrow passages between the islands in front of that
defile) enables the controlling country to prevent our warships
from going from the Black Sea into the Mediterranean, and also
from moving in the opposite direction, either to reinforce our
Black Sea fleet or to find shelter in our Black Sea ports.

If the same country also controls the Bosporus, it can introduce
enemy warships, either its own or those of another nation, from
the Mediterranean into the Black Sea. A stark example of such a
situation, which endangers the defense of our Southern coast, is
the appearance of the *Goeben* and the *Breslau* in the Black Sea.

Accordingly, our strategic goals in regard to the Straits can
be of two kinds.

We can limit our aspirations to the creation of a situation that
would enable us to prevent entrance into the Black Sea of any
alien [war] ship. Such an aim could be called passive defense.

The establishment of such a situation would considerably
strengthen and simplify the defense of the Black Sea coast. It
would enable us to reduce our Black Sea fleet considerably. [That
force's] assignment would then be limited to possible action
against the navy of any of the countries bordering the Black Sea.

In contrast to such a purely defensive aim, a broader aim—so
to speak, an active one—should be considered: namely, securing
free passage of our warships through the Straits at any time, wartime included, and assuring their free sailing into the Mediterranean. This obviously would demand that we be in control of all
of the waterway from the Black Sea into the Mediterranean.

But we should make a reservation: our control of the waterway,
even including the group of Aegean islands in front of the Dardanelles, cannot in all circumstances give us the assurance of a
free exit into the Mediterranean. Obviously an enemy in control
of that sea would always be able to prevent our ships from entering it. Such a situation would unavoidably arise in the course of a
conflict with a first-class sea Power, provided that Power's fleet

was not diverted in a different direction, as for instance would be the case if that Power should simultaneously be in conflict with another important sea Power.

If our warships were assured of a free exit into the Mediterranean, the role of our Black Sea fleet would be completely altered. Its activity would not be limited to the Black Sea. We would be able to use it in other seas. We would not be obliged, as we are now, to maintain considerable naval forces in other seas, a situation which places great stress on our budget. We would in that case have to maintain only one "Fleet of the Open Sea" in the Black Sea, and keep in other seas only limited naval forces assigned exclusively to defensive operations.

Resulting cuts in the naval budget would to some extent compensate the unavoidable financial sacrifices that would be required to consolidate our control over the Straits.

Furthermore, free navigation through the Straits would afford our Navy the opportunity of becoming a menace in the Mediterranean, and that, if we possess important naval forces, would considerably strengthen our influence in the world. As already stated, the Straits are an excellent naval base for operations in the Mediterranean.

Of course the value of these arguments can be vigorously disputed. In particular, one could doubt that a broad, aggressive sea policy would benefit us, at least at the present time.

The main argument for solving the Question of the Straits by securing an exit for our warships into the Mediterranean stems from the consideration that in wartime free exit from the Straits for commercial shipping and warships is determined by exactly the same conditions.

Indeed, should any country make passage from the Black Sea into the Mediterranean factually impossible—for instance, by laying mines in the Dardanelles—then not only would our warships be unable to sail through, but so would the commercial ships of all countries. In the case of a blockade of the Dardanelles, commercial ships would be in the same situation as warships. Freedom of commercial navigation could be assured only by preventing the blockade.

Therefore an active strategic goal regarding the Straits calls for the same solution as the goal of securing an economic exit into the Mediterranean, insofar as we recognize that this exit also should be secure in case of war.

III

Possession of the Straits enables a country to use them in order to prevent navigation from the Black Sea into the Mediterranean and back. As long as they are in the hands of Turkey, the exit of our warships from the Black Sea is inevitably subordinated to her.

But as the situation stands now, exit from the Black Sea is closed to our warships regardless of the Turkish attitude. Treaties now in force stipulate that passage through the Bosporus and the Dardanelles is forbidden to warships of all nations [in time of peace].

This prohibition has been evaluated in various ways from the standpoint of our interests.

The following considerations support the opinion that the legally established closing of the Straits is to our disadvantage.

Firstly, the closing of the Straits deprives Russia at all times, even when at peace with Turkey, of the possibility of moving naval forces from the Black Sea to other seas and back. In 1904 this regulation keeping the Straits closed to warships prevented Russia from using her Black Sea fleet in the war against Japan. It is possible that the outcome of that war was greatly affected by this situation.

Secondly, under this regulation Russia is prevented from using her Black Sea shipyards for the general maintenance of her Navy, because it is impossible for her to move vessels built in the Black Sea into other seas.

Thirdly, the closing of the Straits to warships prevents Russia from reinforcing her Black Sea fleet by any means except building new ships in our Black Sea shipyards. This places us at a disadvantage with respect to possible antagonists in that sea. The purchase by Turkey of ready warships in other countries could tilt the balance of forces in the Black Sea in her favor for a long time, as our only means of counterbalancing such reinforcement of the Turkish fleet would be to build new vessels in our Black Sea shipyards. This would, of course, require a long time. Turkey also could gain advantage over us by ordering warships in the ship-

yards of Western countries, where ships are built much more
rapidly than in ours. Our helpless situation consequent to that
state of affairs became obvious when it was learned that Turkey
had acquired the Brazilian dreadnought *Rio de Janeiro* and ordered in England the dreadnought *Reshada*.

The following arguments are advanced against allowing warships of any nation to pass through the Straits.

It is argued that if we agree to admit alien fleets into the Black
Sea we renounce our exclusive situation in that sea and lose one
of our means of exerting constant pressure on Turkey for the
achievement of our goals in the Near East.

Also, if the Straits stay open, the possibility arises that
permanent alien naval forces may appear in the Black Sea. Unfriendly countries could use this situation to create a constant
threat to Russia.

There also exists an opinion that the decision to keep the
Straits open would compel us to create in advance a powerful
naval force in the Black Sea. This consideration cannot be accepted as valid. It proceeds from the mistaken belief that, because
of the existing treaties which close the Straits, our only potential
enemy in the Black Sea might be Turkey. That such an opinion
can be borne should be regarded as one of the dangerous consequences of the Straits' being closed.

In order to combine the advantages which an opening of the
Straits would bring us with the advantages of keeping the Black
Sea closed to alien fleets, it has been suggested that only warships
of countries having a Black Sea coastline should be allowed to
pass through the Straits. This solution to the problem of alien warships being allowed to pass through the Straits must be considered
the most desirable from our point of view. But acceptance of the
principle of unequal rights for ships sailing under different colors
has little chance for success.

If we weigh all considerations for and against having the Straits
open, we must admit that the advantages offered us by the right
to send our warships through the Straits far outweigh the disadvantages of admitting alien fleets into the Black Sea. Incidentally,
these disadvantages will disappear if the exit from the Bosporus
into the Black Sea falls into our hands.

IV

As already mentioned, the group of Aegean islands lying in front of the Dardanelles—Tenedos, Imbros, Lemnos, and Samothrace—could be used to facilitate operations against the Straits.

The strategic goal of safeguarding our exit into the Mediterranean therefore cannot be achieved without involving these islands.

They are not all of equal tactical value. The freedom of exit from any narrow passage can be secured only by the creation in front of it of a space where a fleet can be deployed before or after using the passage.

Imbros and Tenedos are so close to the mouth of the Dardanelles that they lie within the space needed for deployment according to modern military methods. Therefore, a fully satisfactory organization of the defenses of the Dardanelles demands that these two islands be used for that purpose. They should form the seafront of a fortress whose role would be to protect the mouth of the Dardanelles from enemy attack from the sea. Otherwise, even a relatively small naval force using these islands could blockade the Dardanelles against a very strong enemy. Artillery could be set up on these islands to place the mouth of the Straits under fire.

While Imbros and Tenedos directly dominate the mouth of the Dardanelles, Lemnos and Samothrace [also] command the above-mentioned space indispensable for deployment. Lemnos, in particular, has excellent bays—Mudros, for instance—and could become an important base for a strict blockade of the deployment area. It follows that the defense of the mouth of the Dardanelles can be satisfactorily organized only if Lemnos and Samothrace are not allowed to be used for enemy action against the Straits.

It should be stressed that the importance of Lemnos is in this respect much greater than that of Samothrace. Lemnos directly commands the deployment area in front of the Dardanelles. Samothrace commands only the northern approach to that area, leaving the remaining approaches free. This island therefore is outside the chain of the three islands on which exit from the Dardanelles waterway directly depends.*

V

Possession and control of the Straits by Turkey has for a long time been considered a satisfactory situation for us. It has been stated that Turkey is not strong enough to threaten us and therefore will take our interests into consideration. At the same time, her sovereignty has freed us from the burden of having to protect the Straits. This opinion [at one time] could be strongly supported, but lately it has become less defensible. The internal dissolution of Turkey has reached such a degree that her government has become a tool of foreign influences. Turkey has fallen into the orbit of a group of countries who are our enemies. Under their pressure, Turkey has started to strengthen her armed forces and has adopted an attitude which is a threat to us. The strategic advantages which she has gained through control of the Straits have a strong impact on the situation in the Black Sea. Disregarding our protests, Turkey has again closed the Straits and thus clearly demonstrated how much her free hand over the Bosporus and the Dardanelles is opposed to our interests.

Yet the problem of the eventual fate of the Straits is now brought to the forefront not because we desire it, but because of the increasing incapacity of Turkey to regenerate herself and keep her territories under control.

If we can no longer tolerate Turkey's rule over the Straits, or at least the present unlimited character of that rule, it would be even worse to have the Straits fall into the hands of a powerful nation.

One can predict with assurance that [the establishment of] control over the Straits by any country capable of resisting our demands would unavoidably create a sharp antagonism between that country and Russia. The reasons for this do not reside merely in the fact that permitting control of the Straits to fall into the hands of a powerful country would be equivalent to subordinating

* A more detailed exposition of the military-naval importance of the Aegean islands situated in the near vicinity of the Dardanelles will be found in the attached memorandum by Commander A. D. Bubnov.

the whole economy of our South [to that Power]; nor are these reasons limited to considerations of the strategic advantages which attend the possession of the keys to the Black Sea. It is the geographic location of the Straits that accords their possession its greater value. Control of the Bosporus and the Dardanelles not only opens a door to influence the whole of the Black Sea and the Mediterranean; it also becomes a source of predominance over the Balkan world and Western Asia. Historically, the fate of these countries has always been Russia's major concern.

We obviously must keep a jealous watch over any chance to inherit this most important political base. Therefore it is quite natural that a conviction has taken shape in Russia [to the effect that] our development as a Great Power cannot be achieved without Russian control over the Bosporus and the Dardanelles, and that such is the only possible final solution to the Question of the Straits.

VI

The preceding exposition leads to the conclusion that the Question of the Straits can be definitely solved only by establishing our complete and direct authority over the Bosporus, the Dardanelles, and some of the Aegean islands with a sufficient hinterland to provide for the stability of our possession. Only through this solution can we firmly and definitely attain all our goals on the Straits, i.e., the economic goal and both strategic ones, active and passive. This is the only solution compatible with our position as a Great Power, and it offers us the means of expanding the role of our fatherland in the world.

The establishment of our direct authority could [also] be limited to the Bosporus alone or to any territory necessary for achieving only the passive strategic goal.

The first solution can be called active, the second passive.

When evaluating the importance of bringing the Straits under our control we should not disregard the negative side of the problem.

If control of the Straits will improve the defense of our Southern coast line, it will at the same time constitute a heavy burden in our overall defense system.

The Straits, if approached from the mainland, are in an extremely vulnerable position. A considerable complement of ground forces would be required to organize their defense.

According to competent persons one can assert that for the defense of the Bosporus we would need not less than 150 to 200 million rubles to build fortifications and establish a permanent garrison of not less than two Army corps. If we also take over the Dardanelles, this outlay of founds and the number of troops should be doubled.

Would the value of these territorial acquisitions justify the sacrifices incurred?

Without deciding beforehand what the answer to this extremely complex question should be, it is necessary to stress that the problem has to be approached from different angles, depending on whether we are seeking an active solution of the Question of the Straits or a passive one.

The gain of considerable advantages for our economy as well as for our political and military positions is the ultimate purpose of securing an exit into the Mediterranean. The achievement of these goals should be considered a requirement of our status as a Great Power. Therefore the question whether the sacrifices necessary to effect the active solution of the Question of the Straits are justified, and whether they are within the limits of Russia's strength and financial means, can be answered only from the point of view of the highest state interests.

The problem narrows down considerably when the passive solution alone is explored. Our aim in that case is limited to the non-admission of enemy warships into the Black Sea. The defense of our Southern coast would benefit from it. But this could also be accomplished by other means, such as reinforcement of our Black Sea fleet and its auxiliaries, coastal fortifications, etc. Yet, no matter how desirable it is to safeguard our Black Sea coast, this remains a local problem in our global system of defense. All this has to be taken into consideration; otherwise we might overestimate [the efficacy of] the passive solution to the Question of the Straits. If this solution has only a limited value and its implementation demands considerable sacrifices, its expedience seems doubtful.

In connection with the sacrifices needed to secure our control of the Straits, a question is being asked: couldn't we compensate for the number of troops used for that purpose by reducing the armed forces in our Southern provinces? This has to be answered in the negative. The number of troops stationed in the Odessa Military District cannot be reduced because of the proximity of Rumania. The presence of considerable military forces in the Caucasus is required not only for the protection of our frontier with Turkey; it is also particularly necessary to maintain order in this region because of the pernicious influence of nearby Persia. The protection of our important interests in that country, where disturbances are always possible, also calls for the presence of considerable armed forces in the Caucasus. For all these reasons it is impossible to leave less than the three Army corps stationed in the Caucasus. As to the threat to our frontier in the Caucasus, this depends on the future of Turkey. If the Ottoman Empire did not disintegrate after losing its last territories in Europe as well as the Straits, then it would continue to draw its forces from Anatolia, which is the present source of its supplies, and it would be able to threaten our Caucasus border. [In such a case] Turkey would probably concentrate even more on that border than she does now. If she were to lose her Southern territories—Syria, Mesopotamia, and Arabia—the might of Turkey would of course diminish. Her political and military aims would undergo a change. Should the Armenian provinces of Turkey become independent we would no longer have any frontier in common.

In view of the difficulties and sacrifices connected with the attainment and consolidation of our control of the Straits, a series of less drastic solutions has been suggested. The realization of our control over the waterway can be conceived in various forms. We must evaluate each combination separately, from the point of view of our own interests, and define to what extent they might satisfy all our above-mentioned goals in regard to the Straits.

VII

It has often been said, particularly abroad, that the Question of the Straits could be solved by their so-called neutralization. This would mean the establishment, by means of an international treaty, of a mutual obligation for all Powers not to violate the freedom of navigation through the Straits in time of peace as well as in time of war. In that case navigation through the Straits would enjoy juridical rights similar to those that were established by the Constantinople agreement of 1888 for the Suez Canal. If such a decision were agreed upon, the problem of who is in possession of the Straits need not be mentioned at all. The shores could remain in the hands of Turkey or be transferred partly or entirely to Bulgaria or Greece. The country controlling the shores would be compelled to dismantle all existing fortifications and would be forbidden to erect new ones. The same obligation would apply to the group of islands in the Aegean Sea which command the approaches to the Dardanelles.

If under any circumstances freedom of navigation through the Straits could be secured by their neutralization, this solution should be considered most tempting. It could be realized without any change in the territorial status quo. It would not require of us the special measures or sacrifices connected with a seizure of the Straits.

But this solution is more visionary than realistic.

International guarantees of the inviolable freedom of navigation through the Straits will create only a purely moral obstacle for any country desirous of closing them or using them for hostile actions against us. No legal guarantees alone can be effective against force, and therefore in time of war they would be worthless unless supported by force. The best proof of this is the recent violation by Germany of the neutrality of Belgium.

The particular example to which one usually refers when suggesting neutralization of the Straits, the Suez Canal, is in itself a proof that neutralization is nothing but a fiction. The de facto master of the Suez Canal is England. Being in full control of the sea, England can at any time occupy the Canal with its fleet and put an end to all international guarantees.

Should the Straits be neutralized, their seizure from the sea would be even easier because of the dismantlement of coastal fortifications.

The defenseless Straits would be open first of all to an attack by the nation whose navy controls the sea. But any Power, even a weaker one, would be able to seize the Straits simply by taking the initiative. It would have but to get its fleet into the Straits first and such a Power could close them by placing its main forces in artillery position, by laying mines, by deploying submarines and a squadron of destroyers. Thereafter a landing could be carried out under protection of an artillery barrage and this position could be fortified and held even against a stronger fleet deployed on the other side of the Straits.

If we do not execute that maneuver ourselves, it can be carried out by our enemies, and not only by a Great Power but even by a secondary Mediterranean Power.

The prohibition of fortifications on the shores of the Straits would not prevent the country which controls them from using them to close the passage and to mount hostile actions against us. [Such a prohibition] would merely make it impossible for that country to maintain on the Straits permanent fortifications and other means of defense which can be erected only by years of labor. But whoever has control of the shores can at short notice install coastal artillery, place torpedo tubes on the waterfront, and lay mines in the waterway. It would even be possible, if one were to take appropriate measures, to prepare platforms in advance for heavy guns, etc., and it would be almost impossible to prevent such action. The danger that the shores of the Straits might be used in such a way obviously would be great if they were to belong to a strong nation. It can therefore be surmised that Bulgaria and Greece would be more dangerous for us in that role than Turkey.

An agreed obligation to abstain from blockading the Straits would also be worthless. This obligation would be effective only in the case of a blockade intended against a state whose supremacy as a naval power would not allow such a blockade to be effective.

Neutralization of the Straits can be realized only if it can be protected by force.

Such an effective protection, if the principle of neutralization is consistently carried out, can be conceived only if organized on an international basis. But under prevailing conditions the creation of any effective sanctions seems unattainable.

The opinion has been expressed that the protection of the Straits could be entrusted to an international naval force. First of all, it is unrealistic to assume that all Powers would be willing to deprive themselves of important naval units for permanent assign-

ment to protect the Straits. Probably they would limit their efforts
to maintaining small patrol craft in the Straits, which would not
offer serious guarantees. Besides, whatever the component of this
international squadron—small craft or large dreadnoughts—it
would cease to serve its purpose as soon as an international conflict should occur. Enemy ships then would obviously pursue their
own military aims, regardless of international guarantees. Those
[vessels] stationed inside the Straits could even be used for aggressive action in the Straits themselves, such as suddenly laying
mines, etc. As to the ships of nations not immediately involved in
the conflict, they would only intervene if their intereest in free
navigation through the Straits was sufficiently powerful to [cause
them to] disregard their neutral status. In that case, their intervention would take place even if the Straits had not been neutralized.

Thus neutralization without sanctions or with the threat of international sanctions cannot be accepted as an effective means of securing the freedom of the Straits. It does not remove the possibility of violation in case of a war, even if Russia has no part in
that conflict. Nor does neutralization offer a solution to the problem of defense of the Black Sea. This particular argument against
neutralization should be abandoned if neutralization were to be
effected for the Dardanelles alone, with control of the Bosporus
given to us. Finally, a formal recognition of the international importance of the Straits sets obstacles to the future attainment of
a solution that would be more in keeping with our own exclusive
interests in the Bosporus and the Dardanelles.

VIII

A neutralization protected not by all Powers but only by our
allies, France and England, conjointly with us, should be considered separately. This solution is suggested for the Dardanelles,
with the Bosporus to be in some manner subordinated to our
exclusive authority.

If establishment of our authority over the Dardanelles is for
some reason considered unattainable or unprofitable, such a
compromise must be considered tempting.

Our passive strategic goal would be reached if we obtained the

Bosporus. As to the free exit into the Mediterranean of war and merchant ships, it would be secure owing to the occupation of the Dardanelles defile by the naval forces of England, France, and Russia.

Taking into account the mighty sea power of these nations, an attack on the Straits from the Mediterranean would be excluded. In spite of the absence of fortifications on the Dardanelles, the allied fleet would prevent their occupation by an enemy from the mainland at least until the shores could be taken over by landing forces, which we could easily bring up if we had full control of the Bosporus.*

The weak point of such a solution of the Question of the Straits lies in the fact that it places the defense of our interests in alien hands. It assumes that the present international alliances will remain unaltered, and that our allies are firmly decided to consider any action by any nation against the Straits as a *casus belli*. If any doubt arises concerning either of these two points, the value of the whole combination is destroyed. In view of the tremendous importance which the Question of the Straits has for us, we are bound to strive toward a solution that would be independent of the decisions of other countries. We must construct it on foundations more solid than those which are presently suggested by the constantly changing international situation.

IX

It is also possible to look for a solution of the Question of the Straits in an alliance with Turkey. An attempt in that direction was made in the signing of the Hunkyar Iskelesi treaty. Such a solution conjectures that Turkey will assume the obligation to secure our freedom of exit into the Mediterranean for both commercial and war ships, and will close the Straits to alien ships at our request. This obviously is worthless unless we are given the means to protect ourselves against any violation of our interests in the Straits, insofar as this is possible while they are not under our direct control. [That protection] could be achieved if we were

* The action of defending the Straits by naval forces is described in detail when the hypothesis of an "occupation of the Straits by naval forces" is examined.

to be given control over the defenses of the Straits and the Turkish navy. Our officers and noncommissioned officers could be introduced into the Straits fortifications in the guise of instructors. The plans for the defense of the Straits should be the responsibility of our General Staff. As to the subordination of the Turkish fleet to our naval mission, this is an absolutely necessary condition, because if the Turkish navy remains independent, our control of the Straits is reduced to zero. Turkish ships stationed in the Straits can at any time open fire on the forts of the Bosporus and Dardanelles from the rear, and can take them over by threatening to do this. Furthermore, it is unrealistic to expect that our officers could force Turkish soldiers to take action against the Turkish fleet.

In order to strengthen our influence it would be further necessary to establish a military mission that could control the whole of the Turkish army. An independent Turkish army might become a tool of influences hostile to our interests. The introduction of Russian instructorship might diminish that danger.

Considerations in favor of this solution list the following advantages: it does not drastically upset the existing situation; it does not involve the question of Constantinople, and it does not require us to face the sacrifices which would become inevitable if we seized the Straits.

But this solution has to be viewed as a half measure. No matter how our control might be organized, the resulting situation would be precarious. This solution would force us always to be prepared to make any move necessary to secure our interests in the Straits, and to plan a strategic operation for their seizure. We would have to keep permanent military and naval contingents ready for such an operation, as well as means for their transportation.

Only the existence of such a constant threat could keep Turkey under our influence, because a number of forces would press that country to free herself from this subordination. Even if the Turkish government should remain unable to act openly in that direction, various Turkish parties and organizations would strive toward it and would find active support outside of Turkey.

Also, putting the control system into practice would not be an easy task. Unfailing vigilance would be necessary to assure its success, and it would greatly depend on the practical means employed. The situation thus created could be a difficult and delicate one, and the personnel in charge necessarily would have to possess certain qualities: tact, adaptability, and experience. It is doubtful that we could organize that aspect in a satisfactory way. The experience of our instructorship in Bulgaria, in Korea, etc., does not afford us any basis for favorable conclusions.

X

To avoid the erection of shore fortifications on the Straits and their inevitable seizure, a solution has been suggested: it can be labelled "occupation of the Straits by naval forces." Following this suggestion, the Question of the Straits would result in an active solution.

The shores of the Straits in this case could remain in the hands of Turkey. She would be obligated to dismantle all fortifications and forbidden to erect new ones. Morover, Turkey would grant us the right to keep our fleet stationed in both straits and to use strongpoints which would not need land defenses but would provide anchorage and depots for coal and other supplies. It would also be to our advantage to obtain the right to use the Marmara islands as strongpoints. There our fleet would be less vulnerable to attack from the mainland. The operational base for our fleet would remain on the Black Sea coast.

The basic idea of this project is to use the fleet as a fortress until the shores can be seized by a landing force.

It is true that the shores of the Straits can be defended for about 20 versts * inland by a fleet's artillery. This type of defense could be but temporary, however, for by a systematic action of the kind used in the siege of fortresses it would be possible to force the fleet out of the Straits. An example of such operations of siege artillery against warships can be found in the action of the Japanese at Port Arthur. There our fleet was first forced out of the harbor by 11-inch guns and then destroyed on its return. In order to prevent the enemy from consolidating his position on the shores and installing heavy artillery against our fleet, it would be necessary to forestall such action by a landing operation. This operation should be sufficiently spread out along the coasts of the

* One *versta* was equal to 0.66 mile. (Editor's note.)

Straits to protect them by means of a field war. The presence of our Navy in the Straits would give us sufficient time and facilities to execute a landing operation. Therefore, for this solution we must have in permanent readiness a landing ground force and transports for moving it, as well as the artillery and engineering forces needed to organize a fortified area (with fortifications of a temporary character) which would secure our possession of the Straits.

In case of enemy action against the Straits from the sea, only part of our naval forces would remain in the Straits—a reserve squadron that would defend the shores. The main forces would advance out of the Straits for purely naval action.

As has already been explained, insofar as our objective in the Straits goes beyond a purely defensive position, and our intention is to secure our freedom of exit into the Mediterranean, it is mandatory that the group of Aegean islands lying in front of the Dardanelles not be allowed to serve either as a naval base for a strict blockade of the Straits, or as a fortified position that can prevent exit from the Straits.

In the case of a solution of the Question of the Straits exclusively by naval forces, the condition just mentioned can be achieved only to a certain extent, and that by imposing on these islands obligations that would prohibit all measures that might render these islands usable for naval military purposes. To this should be added authorization for us to have an anchorage base on Tenedos or Imbros. It has also been pointed out that we could establish a fortified naval base on one of these islands. This measure must be considered of little avail, for as long as we do not control the shores of the Straits the communications between such a base and our rear cannot be sufficiently secured.

So far as Turkey is concerned, such a solution offers us a means of exerting pressure through the constant threat to Constantinople which the presence of our fleet will pose. But [to meet all eventualities] it would be preferable to have the Turkish ground and naval forces under our control; otherwise they might obstruct our actions inside the Straits as well as outside them.

Occupation of the Straits by naval forces would be only a preliminary solution to the question. It would not relieve us of the necessity, in case of complications, to follow up with a seizure of the shores of the Straits, and it would oblige us to be ever ready for a landing operation. It would not completely secure our control of the Straits. By rapid action and with some luck, an enemy could force our fleet out of the Straits before the arrival of our landing forces, and even after our landing he could hope for success in a field war. One should not expect that a firm defense system could be rapidly organized on the shores. Considering the power of modern artillery, fortifications can be efficient only when built of concrete. Building them is of course possible only when the territory to be defended remains for a long time in the same hands. Nor does this solution offer us means to avoid important material sacrifice. It presupposes constant readiness of a landing army as well as of transportation means, and it ties up considerable naval forces in the Straits.

One could mention that if the suggestion of "occupation of the Straits by naval forces" were to be applied only to the Dardanelles, it might be a useful addition to the solution which limited our complete domination to the Bosporus. It would enable us, to a certain extent at least, to combine with the latter the realization of our active goals in the Straits if we possessed a firm base in the closest rear of the Dardanelles, their occupation by our naval forces would also be facilitated.

XI

As we move to those solutions of the Question of the Straits which deal with our seizure of territory on the shores of that waterway, we must first of all examine the suggestions whose aim is only to secure the defense of the Black Sea. This is a passive strategic goal.

In this respect it would seem appropriate to start with the opinion that the defense of the Black Sea can be assured by our acquiring a naval base on the Black Sea coast in the vicinity of the Bosporus instead of seizing the shores of the Straits. It has been pointed out that in this case it would become possible to achieve a tight blockade of the mouth of the Bosporus. This would be a difficult operation now, because of the great distance between Sebastopol and the entrance into the Black Sea.

Possession of such a base would indeed greatly improve the

strategic position of our Black Sea fleet. It would permit our fleet to maintain a constant observation of the mouth of the Bosporus and would prevent enemy ships from entering into the Black Sea without doing battle. As long as there are no [enemy] fortifications adequate to create a satisfactory deployment area in front of the Bosporus, a battle at the mouth of the Bosporus will offer considerable tactical advantages to our Navy.

But in that case the defense of the Black Sea would depend solely on the outcome of a naval engagement. This would always be unpredictable, and hence in this case the defense of the Black Sea could not be considered secure. Another reason why the idea of solving our problems in this matter should be dropped is that a naval base by the Bosporus would need the protection of a large fortress; the sacrifices required for construction of such a fortress could be justified only if it offered a more satisfactory solution to the problem of keeping the Black Sea closed. Besides, the only two bays situated in the vicinity of the Bosporus—Iniada and Bender-Eregli—cannot be used for naval bases; the former because it has no suitable conditions for anchorage, the latter because it is too small.

In order to limit as much as possible the territory we would occupy and to avoid including Constantinople in that territory, it has been suggested, at least for an early period, that the group of Marmara islands * should be handed over to us, and also, if possible, the Artaki (or Kapu-Dag) peninsula with the stipulation that all the fortifications of the Bosporus will be dismantled. Thus our defense of the Black Sea would be moved to a line connecting the northern shore of the Sea of Marmara with its southern shore, and passing through the Marmara islands. A fortified naval base would have to be constructed on these islands. The defense would be carried out by the active forces of the fleet. The advantages of this position, which would offer us the possibility of making full use of submarines, mine belts, and shore artillery on the island of Marmara, would enable our fleet to withstand the attack of even superior naval forces. Dismantling the fortifications on the Bosporus, and more important still, the possibility of our threatening

* This group of islands is to be understood to include the following: Marmara, Athizia, and Aloni (or Pasha Liman), and smaller islands lying close to them.

the Turkish capital at any time, would to a certain extent secure communications with the Black Sea and our ports.

It is evident that this solution has much in common with the plan designated "occupation of the Straits by naval forces" and could be considered supplemental to it. The [two plans] have many common weak points. Neither of them can relieve us of the necessity of [preparing] a landing operation to counter a threat from the mainland. Neither offers a satisfactory guarantee to our positions. We cannot exclude the possibility that an enemy fleet could, with some luck, break through the Sea of Marmara defense line. The defense of the Black Sea cannot be considered sufficiently secure if this solution is adopted; the same can be said of the communication line between our base and the rear.

The only advantage of this solution when compared with those discussed earlier is that it offers us a somewhat more secure situation, thanks to the fortified position we would obtain in the Straits. Yet this fortified position is not completely adequate to the defense task it is meant to carry out.

The solution just discussed should be accepted only if it should prove impossible for us to take possession of the shores of the Bosporus.

There was a time when it was considered possible to secure the defense of the Black Sea by the occupation of the Upper Bosporus only. It was on that basis that our Administration planned to solve the Question of the Straits in the last decade of the last century. It was planned that we would limit our occupation along the Bosporus to positions up to Beykoz on the Asiatic shore and to Kierech-Burnu on the European shore. Such a decision would be tempting because it would permit us to avoid the problem of Constantinople. But in our time, possession of the Upper Bosporus alone is definitely insufficient. The action of modern long-range artillery would annihilate our few forts on the shores of the Upper Bosporus in the very first days of a war.

Full control of the Bosporus can be firmly in our hands only if we possess both shores of the Straits with enough depth of territory to enable us to build a major fortress equal to all modern technical demands.

Topography considerations decree that the best position for the defense of the Bosporus on the side of the Thracian peninsula is the Tchataldja position *, which extends from the bay of Buyuk-Chekmedje to Derkos Lake, while on the side of the Bithynian peninsula the best position would be that which commands Sabandja Lake and goes along the Sakaria River and then from the mouth of this river to Ismit. These defense lines should form the front of our permanent fortifications. A necessary condition for satisfactory organization of their defense would be the occupation of a sufficiently wide stretch of land beyond these lines. Possession of land in front of the fortress is necessary in order to keep under observation the zone from which the fortress might be fired upon, and for securing a deployment area where troops defending the fortress would have freedom for tactical movements. The troops also should have space for advantageous advanced positions. In short, the defense should be able to be as active as possible and because of that to last longer and be successful. This area definitely should not be less than 20 versts wide, but in view of the progress of military technique it would be preferable to make it wider. At present, we usually consider that a fortress area should extend 30 to 40 versts in front of the fortified line. The Princes' Islands should be inside the occupied territory. They should be included in the seafront of the fortress. In spite of their location, which is not satisfactory for protection of the deployment area in front of the mouth of the Bosporus, they could nevertheless to some extent facilitate the exit of our fleet into the Sea of Marmara.

As was mentioned earlier, the approximate cost of building such a fortress can be estimated at 150 to 200 million rubles. As to the garrison, it should comprise not less than two Army corps.

The erection of a vast fortress that would include in its boundaries the city of Constantinople, does not imply the necessity of having that city under our full administrative control. The civil administration inside the city boundaries could be organized on a basis of autonomy, and our interference could be limited to our specifically military interests. Constantinople would be subordinated to our military government only if it happened that the territory under occupation should be in a state of siege. Granting self-government to the city of Constantinople would lessen the

* The position of Makriki is less convenient for defense and certainly does not project forward sufficiently.

frictions that would be unavoidable if we were to establish a direct influence over such an important center in which so many interests—financial, national, religious, and others—are concentrated. It would [also] offer some satisfaction to Hellenism, which so jealously watches all our moves in the direction of this historic city.

Our occupation should not be limited to one shore of the Bosporus. The construction of a fortress protecting only one side of these Straits would cost as much money and demand as many troops as a fortress extending on both shores up to the favorable defense lines described above. If we were to occupy only one shore, our defenses would not be as reliable as those which could be erected if we occupied both shores. A coast of the Bosporus not firmly in our hands could be utilized by an enemy as a convenient position for action against our fortress. Also, if we were to control only one shore, the waterway could be placed under enemy attack and our fleet could be deprived of its base. The fleet would be unable to support the fortress from the Sea of Marmara side. A breakthrough of the enemy fleet into the Black Sea would then be possible, and this would also endanger communication lines between the fortress and the rear. For all these reasons, if danger should arise the unfortified shore of the Bosporus would still have to be occupied by us, but defending it by means of field-war action would be more difficult than if it had been included within the fortress boundary.

In order to reinforce the defense of the Bosporus, it would be highly desirable if we could complement the erection of a fortress by an occupation of the Marmara islands and include with them, if possible, the Artaki (Kapu-Dag) peninsula. The Marmara islands afford a good position for action against the Bosporus. If we establish a fortress on these Straits it is mandatory that we be protected from any attempt to utilize these islands for hostile actions against us. On the other hand, as stated above, possession of the Marmara islands would allow us to create a protective naval line in front of the Straits which could prevent an enemy fleet from penetrating into the eastern part of the Sea of Marmara. This possibility of preventing enemy naval forces from reaching the Upper Bosporus would safeguard our fortress from artillery fire directed on its flanks from the sea, and would particularly pro-

tect our position at Tchataldja. Moreover if our defense line is
more distant from the Bosporus, Constantinople would be protected from the threat of bombardment inasmuch as that city, even
if granted autonomy, would still be considered under our military protection. A forward line of defense for the fortress on the
Marmara islands would also be the best solution to the problem
of securing an exit for our fleet from the Bosporus into the Sea
of Marmara.

If a completely efficient passive solution of the Question of the
Straits requires extension of our occupation not only over the
Bosporus but also over the Marmara islands, there remains but
one more step to an active solution. This step will be the easier
to take [if one considers that] the advantages stemming from
the active solution far outweigh the results obtained by the passive one.

XII

An active solution of the Question of the Straits can be assured
only if we obtain possession of the Dardanelles defile. As already
stated, this area includes not only the narrows between the penin-
sulas of Gallipoli and Troy, but also all the expanse of sea between the narrows and the islands of Tenedos, Imbros, Lemnos,
and Samothrace. Seizure of all the territories adjacent to the Dardanelles defile and their transformation into a vast fortified region
of course would be ideal for establishing our predominance over
the area. But such a large-scale solution to our problem would be
rather difficult to realize.

The defense of the Dardanelles from the mainland would certainly be much easier if the narrows were in the rear of a fortress
covering both shores. But because of the configuration of the
Asiatic shore of the Dardanelles and the topography of its surface,
the southern front of the fortress would have to be projected forward to include all of the peninsula of Troy. Construction of
a fortress with such a large periphery would entail excessive
sacrifices. Therefore it would be more realistic to limit oneself to
construction of a powerful fortress on the Gallipoli peninsula. The
southern front of this fortress, together with the fleet and the
support of the fortress garrison, would protect the Straits from

any attack coming from Asia Minor. The decision to leave the southern shore of the Dardanelles unfortified could to some degree be compensated by the creation of conditions which would hamper enemy activity there. For that purpose it would be necessary to extend the right to utilize the southern shore of the Dardanelles for military objectives, and, if possible, the whole Trojan peninsula up to the Adramiti-Pandarma line as well. Possession of the Asiatic shore of the Straits would also enable preparation of a deployment area for the protection of the approaches to the straits from Asia Minor. This could be done with field army forces. If worst comes to worst, we could be satisfied with a limitation on alien territorial predominance over this shore, at least as far as the Eski-Stambul cape. This limitation would consist in an obligation to dismantle all fortifications and abstain from building military installations and strategic roads, etc., and in general from using this territory for military purposes. We should have the right to supervise the execution of these measures of neutralization.

The protection of the Gallipoli peninsula from the mainland side would be completely secure if we were to fortify the excellent position at Bolayir. Beyond that fortification we should expand our occupation over a stretch 20 versts wide—even better, 30 or 40 versts—in order to create in front of the fortress a deployment area needed for the same reasons as were stated in describing the building of a fortress on the Bosporus.

As already stated when the tactical importance of the group of Aegean islands adjacent to the Dardanelles was discussed, a fortress whose aim is to secure the exit from the Straits cannot be organized in a satisfactory manner unless the islands of Imbros and Tenedos are included in its seafront life. Artillery must be placed on these islands. Possession of these islands is therefore an absolute condition.*

As to Lemnos and Samothrace, considerations stated earlier show that they could be utilized to threaten navigation along the waterways leading from the mouth of the Dardanelles to the sea. This menace can best be removed if we gain possession of both islands. It is particularly desirable that we obtain Lemnos, which

* Possession of Tenedos obviously involves occupation of the small island of Rabit, which lies between Tenedos and the Dardanelles and could also be utilized for military purposes.

represents a position of greater importance than Samothrace. In
that case we would have complete mastery over the northeastern
corner of the Aegean Sea, and any blockade of the Straits would
become such a complicated operation that it would have little
effect. The possession of Lemnos would be useful even if we did
not build a fortress there. The use of this position for purely naval
action would enable us to expand to the utmost the scope of our
fleet operations, and consequently would create the best possible
conditions for the defense of our position. Therefore we can renounce Lemnos only under pressure of absolute necessity. If it
becomes impossible for us to obtain Lemnos and Samothrace, we
could accept a situation which leaves them in the hands of a
second-rate power (for instance Greece, which already occupies
them), but in that case their neutralization should be an absolute
condition, i.e., they must be kept without fortifications and under
interdiction of any construction for military naval purposes. This
situation would not prevent us from temporarily taking over
Lemnos—in case of emergency—and using it for our needs. But
the transfer of Lemnos into the hands of a Great Power and its
transformation into a base for a powerful fleet, would greatly reduce the importance of our [proposed] fortress on the Dardanelles.
An opinion has been voiced on this subject to the effect that
we should permit only a first-rate naval Power to have possession
of Lemnos because in any case we would not be able to challenge
[such a Power] at sea or to protect our trade from it. This consideration, as stated earlier, is valid only as long as the navy of
this Power is not engaged in another area. If occupied elsewhere,
even that Power would be unable to carry out the blockade of the
vast maritime region protected by Lemnos.

The importance of Lemnos as a position which threatens the
route from the Straits into the sea could be reduced by a canal dug
across the Gallipoli peninsula. In that case Samothrace would acquire part of the strategic importance which now belongs to Lemnos. Our occupation of Samothrace together with the creation of a
new exit into the sea through the Gulf of Saros could to a certain
extent offset the effects of any conversion of Lemnos into an alien
naval base.

According to an approximate estimate, the cost of building a
fortress on the Gallipoli peninsula with the inclusion of a seafront

formed by artillery batteries on Imbros and Tenedos, would amount to 150 to 200 million rubles; a permanent garrison of not less than two Army corps would be necessary for its defense.

A fortified position on the Dardanelles would require adequate security of communications with the rear defense situated on our Black Sea coast. The importance of security for such communications would be increased by the high cost of such a fortress and the sizable garrison it would require. Therefore, occupation of the Dardanelles without fortification of the Bosporus must be considered unsatisfactory. Posession of both shores of the Bosporus would in this case be particularly necessary to ensure absolute security of communications by sea from the Marmara to the Black Sea. In order to improve communications, it would be advisable to occupy also the islands of Marmara and the Artaki (or Kapu-Dag) peninsula. This occupation would eliminate the danger of having the islands used against us as a position dominating the exit from the Dardanelles into the Sea of Marmara. It would doubtless be more convenient to establish a naval base on these islands than to have it in the Dardanelles, particularly if only one shore of the straits is to be fortified.

One has to mention here the opinion that, because fortifications on the Dardanelles would be much more important to us than occupation of the Bosporus, we could build them without being masters of the latter, provided the general situation is such that our communications between the Dardanelles and the Black Sea are not greatly endangered. This presupposes that the shores of the Bosporus and of the Sea of Marmara will not, under any circumstances, fall into the hands of a stronger nation; that the capital of Turkey will remain in Constantinople and therefore under the menace of our fleet; that there will be no fortifications on the shores of the Bosporus; that the Turkish fleet will be either moved and stationed to the west of the Dardanelles or placed under our effective control; that we will be masters of the Marmara Islands; and finally, that the interdiction of passage through the Straits will remain in force for the navies of all nations except those having a coastline on the Black Sea. Even so, in case of danger to our communication line we would be obliged to dispatch a landing force and occupy the shores of the Bosporus immediately. It is hard to see how the communication line between our Dardanelles fortress and the Black Sea ports could be considered secure under these circumstances.

The defense of the Dardanelles and Bosporus positions could be made even more secure through our occupation of all the shores of the Sea of Marmara, both south and north, or only one of them. A vast deployment area would enable us to conduct a more active defense and at the same time to establish a route of communication by land between the two fortresses. But not only might such an expansion of our occupation arouse political difficulties, it would have still another negative aspect: we would have to increase our occupation army in proportion to the lengthening of our front line.

The threat to the Straits being greater from the European mainland, it would be most profitable to expand our occupation in that direction. An ideal solution would be to include in our occupation territory all the Thracian valley, including Adrianople. Also a most satisfactory position for defense would be obtained by an extention of our occupation up to the line going from Enes along the Maritza and Ergene rivers approximately as far as Luleburgas and from there toward Midye. In that case we would have at our disposal a range of parallel defense lines on gentle slopes between the riverbeds of the tributaries of the Ergene River.

Should it be impossible to extend our occupation over the whole coastline of the Sea of Marmara, or should it be considered undesirable that we do so, it will become necessary to protect our sea communication lines from an eventual threat from alien naval forces. Even an insignificant fleet with a base between the two straits could, if protected by the forts of that base, become a serious impediment for us. Therefore the conditions under which we can permit the shores of the Sea of Marmara to be in alien hands should be that there would be no alien fortified naval base on these shores, and no permanent alien naval forces in these waters, or at least no forces of unlimited size.

If we do not occupy the northern coast of the Marmara Sea ourselves, it might be suggested that it be given over to Bulgaria as a compensation for her help. It would be preferable to avoid giving Bulgaria access to the Sea of Marmara, as this would mean an extra threat for us in that sea. But if the rights of Bulgaria on that sea and its shores were to be limited as described above, we could agree to that concession as a last resort. But if we occupy only the Bosporus, Bulgarian access to the Sea of Marmara must be judged definitely undesirable. In the hands of Bulgaria, Rodosto could become a base for action not only against the Bosporus but even against our navigation through the Dardanelles. For us this danger would increase if Bulgaria were to side with an important naval Power who is our enemy.

*   *   *

For the compilation of this memorandum I received information on military matters from the quartermaster general, General of the Infantry Iu. N. Danilov; on naval-military matters I received data from the chief of the operations section for the Black Sea fleet at the Naval General Staff, Commander A. V. Nemits, and Commander A. D. Bubnov. I also used the military geographical works published by Major-General Kholmsen and Colonel Gudim-Levkovich, as well as various materials housed at the Naval General Staff and the Ministry of Foreign Affairs.

November 1914

N. Bazili

Appendix II

Appendix

Act of Abdication

Signed by Nicholas II

General Headquarters

To the Chief of Staff

In the days of great struggle with an external foe, who has been striving for almost three years to enslave our native land, it has been God's will to visit upon Russia a new grievous trial. The internal disturbances which have begun among the people threaten to have a calamitous effect on the future conduct of a hard-fought war. The destiny of Russia, the honor of our heroic army, the welfare of the people, the whole future of our beloved fatherland demand that the war be carried to a victorious conclusion no matter what the cost. The cruel foe is straining his last resources and the time is already close at hand when our valiant army, together with our glorious allies, will be able to crush the foe completely. In these decisive days in the life of Russia, We have deemed it Our duty in conscience to help Our people to draw closer together and to unite all the forces of the nation for a speedier attainment of victory, and, in agreement with the State Duma, We have judged it right to abdicate the Throne of the Russian State and to lay down the Supreme Power. Not wishing to be parted from Our beloved Son, We hand over Our succession to Our Brother, the

187

Grand Duke Mikhail Alexandrovich, and bless Him on his accession to the Throne of the Russian State. We enjoin Our Brother to conduct the affairs of the state in complete and inviolable union with the representatives of the people in the legislative bodies on the principles to be established by them, and to take an inviolable oath to this effect. In the name of the dearly beloved native land, We call upon all true sons of the Fatherland to fulfill their sacred duty to It by their obedience to the Tsar at this time of national trial and to help Him, together with the people's representatives, to lead the Russian State onto the path of victory, prosperity, and glory. May the Lord God help Russia!

Nicholas

Pskov, March 2, 1917, 3:00 p.m.

Minister of the Imperial Court, Chief-Aide-de-Camp Count Fredericks

Ставка

Начальнику Штаба.

Въ дни великой борьбы съ внѣшнимъ врагомъ, стремящимся почти три года поработить нашу родину Господу Богу угодно было ниспослать Россіи новое тяжкое испытаніе. Начавшіяся внутреннія народныя волненія грозятъ бѣдственно отразиться на дальнѣйшемъ веденіи упорной войны. Судьба Россіи, честь геройской нашей арміи, благо народа, все будущее дорогого нашего Отечества требуютъ доведенія войны во что бы то ни стало до побѣднаго конца. Жестокій врагъ напрягаетъ послѣднія силы и уже близокъ часъ, когда доблестная армія наша совмѣстно со славными нашими союзниками сможетъ окончательно сломить врага. Въ эти рѣшительные дни въ жизни Россіи, почли МЫ долгомъ совѣсти облегчить народу НАШЕМУ тѣсное единеніе и сплоченіе всѣхъ силъ народныхъ для скорѣйшаго достиженія побѣды и, въ согласіи съ Государственною Думою, признали МЫ за благо отречься отъ Престола Государства Россійскаго и сложить съ СЕБЯ Верховную власть. Не желая разстаться съ любимымъ Сыномъ НАШИМЪ, МЫ передаемъ наслѣдіе НАШЕ Брату НАШЕМУ Великому Князю МИХАИЛУ АЛЕКСАНДРОВИЧУ и благословляемъ Его на вступленіе на Престолъ Государства Россійскаго. Заповѣдуемъ Брату НАШЕМУ править дѣлами государственными въ полномъ и ненарушимомъ единеніи съ представителями народа въ законодательныхъ учрежденіяхъ, на тѣхъ началахъ, кои будутъ ими установлены, принеся въ томъ ненарушимую присягу. Во имя горячо любимой родины призываемъ всѣхъ вѣрныхъ сыновъ Отечества къ исполненію своего святого долга передъ Нимъ, повиновеніемъ Царю въ тяжелую минуту всенародныхъ испытаній и помочь ЕМУ, вмѣстѣ съ представителями народа, вывести Государство Россійское на путь побѣды, благоденствія и славы. Да поможетъ Господь Богъ Россіи.

Г. Псковъ.

2 Марта 15 час. мин. 1917 г.

Министръ Императорскаго Двора
Генералъ Адъютантъ Графъ Фредериксъ

Николай

Act of Abdication as signed by Nicolas II.

Index

191